Righteous Riches

The Word of Faith Movement in
Contemporary African American Religion

MILMON F. HARRISON

OXFORD
UNIVERSITY PRESS

2005

OXFORD
UNIVERSITY PRESS

Oxford University Press, Inc., publishes works that further
Oxford University's objective of excellence
in research, scholarship, and education.

Oxford   New York
Auckland   Cape Town   Dar es Salaam   Hong Kong   Karachi
Kuala Lumpur   Madrid   Melbourne   Mexico City   Nairobi
New Delhi   Shanghai   Taipei   Toronto

With offices in
Argentina   Austria   Brazil   Chile   Czech Republic   France   Greece
Guatemala   Hungary   Italy   Japan   Poland   Portugal   Singapore
South Korea   Switzerland   Thailand   Turkey   Ukraine   Vietnam

Copyright © 2005 by Oxford University Press, Inc.

Published by Oxford University Press, Inc.
198 Madison Avenue, New York, New York 10016
www.oup.com

Oxford is a registered trademark of Oxford University Press

Library of Congress Cataloging-in-Publication Data
Harrison, Milmon F.
   Righteous riches : the Word of faith movement in contemporary African
American religion / Milmon F. Harrison.
      p. cm.
   Includes bibliographical references and index.
   ISBN-13 978-0-19-515313-2; 978-0-19-515388-0 (pbk.)
   ISBN 0-19-515313-8; 0-19-515388-X (pbk.)
   1. African Americans—Religion.   2. Faith movement (Hagin).   I. Title.
   BR563.N4H378 2005
   277.3'083'08996073—dc22   2004017069

9 8 7 6 5 4 3

Printed in the United States of America
on acid-free paper

This book is dedicated to my wife,
Suzette Denise Harrison

Preface

I did not grow up "in church," as part of a formal religious body like many of my closest African American friends and acquaintances. As one who came to organized religion in my mid-twenties, I found that there was much to learn that so many of those in my immediate circle already knew and took for granted. In early 1987 I was a new convert beginning the process of socialization into the world of Christianity in a Word of Faith Movement church. This was the same church in Sacramento, California, that serves as the backdrop for this book. As an excited, born again, "baby" Christian (as new converts are often referred to), I spent many hours in church services, Bible studies, and other structured activities learning the basics of Christian belief and practice. During this period of acculturation into this subculture I also learned what was expected of me in my new role as "church member." I served as a volunteer in the ministry in a number of capacities, spending innumerable hours working, and in the process I learned the culture of my local church and the larger movement from the inside out and came to identify myself as part of this world. The Word of Faith Movement and the Faith Message in my local church formed my first impression of what it actually meant to live a Christian life. It was there that I met, and later married, my wife. A few years later, as an undergraduate sociology major at the University of California, Davis, I found that my experience as a church member shaped my interest in the sociological study of religion. I had to look no further than my own community of faith as I began to formulate the research questions that eventually led to my doctoral dissertation and this book.

But although I have personal knowledge and "insider" experience with the Word of Faith Movement and the local church that served as the setting for this book, my intention was not to write an exposé of the movement, its doctrine, or its members or leaders. There are plenty of other places for readers to go if that is what they are seeking. Rather this book is my attempt to initiate constructive inquiry into a contemporary religious movement that has received a considerable amount of attention in the popular Christian press while, for some reason, scholars of religion have left it relatively untouched. The target audience for this book is the reader who is not an expert in this area of study but who is, nevertheless, interested in learning more about the movement without being subjected to a theological apologia or a delineation of the ways it is doctrinally in error. For this reason some of my observations have been written less for sake of argumentation or to advance sociological theory, than to help expose the reader to some of the details about this movement, its doctrines, and some of its most prominent figures. Many of these are recognizable personalities readers may have already encountered via the broadcast media but until now have not had the larger context in which to place them. The aim of this book is to provide such a context.

A major goal of this book is to provide a venue for the opinions and perspectives of "ordinary" members of a congregation within the larger Word of Faith Movement to speak on various issues concerning their own faith and their application of it. I wanted readers to be able to gain insight into the ways members actively struggle to make meaning of their beliefs and what they are being taught, in the context of their everyday experience. In the daily round of everyday experience is where religion loses its abstraction and becomes real for its adherents. For this reason, I have limited abstract theoretical discussions and tried to write in language that is straightforward, clear, and as free of sociological jargon as possible. As a researcher and a writer, the accessibility of my work to as broad an audience as possible is an important part of my values and my politics, and I hope that I have remained true to both.

Finally, although I am no longer a member of a Word of Faith Movement congregation as I was when I began this research, having been a member has been at once an asset and a liability. My relative insider status provided access and a certain degree of insight into the world about which I have written. Along with those I interviewed for the book, I have personally lived and witnessed many of the types of things I have written about here even before becoming a sociologist. But just as much as it has *helped* me in this project, my insider status has also been a hindrance inasmuch as it produced in me a strong emotional reaction to some discoveries about the movement, and especially about the local congregation of which I was a member for more than a decade. I have strong affective ties to the Movement; there are many people I love and respect that are still part of it, and I found myself wanting to shield them from embarrassment or ridicule from potential detractors. I found myself at various points along the way quite ambivalent about this project and its direction, wanting to avoid certain issues altogether while overemphasizing others. But in the midst of this internal struggle (which continues today, I might add), I reminded myself that I have to do nothing more than tell the truth as I see, hear, and understand it. So this project has led me on a long, arduous journey of self-discovery in addition to furthering my academic and professional re-search goals.

As a sociologist *and* a believer, I find myself in what sometimes feels like a precarious position. I am aware that my work might affect what some readers think about Christianity in general or the Word of Faith Movement, for better or worse. With this book I have attempted to show that human interaction and collective activity—situated and embedded in specific socio-cultural, economic, political, historical, and, of course, spiritual *contexts*—give religion its meaning for those who make up communities of faith based on any particular set of beliefs and practices. Whether I have attained this goal will be for the reader to judge.

For helping to make this book possible I would like to first thank my family, whether by blood or by love. Without your aid, support, encouragement, and prayers this book might not have been. Over the years the awesome power of your high expectations for me have both motivated and sustained me. I thank my dissertation committee in the Department of Sociology at the University of California, Santa Barbara: Professors Wade Clark Roof, Harvey Molotch, and Mark Juergensmeyer as well as Professor Lyn Lofland in the Department of Sociology at the University of California, Davis. My gratitude to you all for guiding me through this process and helping me turn such an important part of my own experience into a long term research project and doctoral degree.

In the years since beginning my college career there have been many people who have provided direction or helped make the way a little easier in some way or another. I am grateful to you all, but I owe a special debt of gratitude to Tonie Hilligoss, my "Introduction to Sociology" instructor at Sac-ramento City College. She was the one who intervened in the trajectory of my life by taking me aside and encouraged me to go to graduate school and work toward becoming a college instructor. When I was a student in her class I was working a full-time day job and attending school full-time at night. She has encouraged and supported me throughout this long process, demonstrating what mentoring looks like by example. I also owe a special debt to former teachers and now colleagues Dr. Jacob K. Olupona, Dr. Moradewun Adejunmobi, Dr. John O. Stewart, and Dr. Patricia Turner of the African American & African Studies Program at the University of California, Davis. Thank you for your continued support and guidance, especially now that I'm one of the "new kids" in our Program. To my other colleagues in the African American & African Studies Program, including the Staff in Hart Hall Interdisciplinary Programs, I also owe my thanks for your continued support and encouragement.

As I worked my way through school in a number of nonacademic jobs, I have been most fortunate to have worked under wonderfully generous managers, supervisors, and co-workers, and I have made life-long friends who continue to enrich my life. Those who gave me work and allowed me to make a living by working around my school schedule at the Safeway warehouse in Sacramento and at the State of California Employment Development Department (EDD) in Sacramento *and* in Santa Barbara, I salute you. We laughed, ate, and worked together. We kept each other going through some pretty rough times and, as promised, I haven't forgotten you. Thank you for encouraging me to keep pursuing my education even when I wanted to give up.

There are many others I should and would like to thank here that space would not permit. I thank my church family at Center of Praise International Ministries, Sacramento, California, and the friends who continue to laugh, cry, pray, and support my family and me in our daily walk. A special thanks goes to Cynthia Read, and all the staff at Oxford University Press who worked on this project. I have an even greater degree of respect now for the process of publishing than when we first began working together. Most of all, I thank all of the people who shared their experiences with me in the interviews that were the basis for this book. Literally, without your help this would not have been possible.

Contents

Righteous Riches

Introduction

The Word of Faith Movement

Beloved, I wish above all things that thou mayest prosper and be in
health, Even as thy soul prospereth.

—3 John 2:2

The world outside swelters this late-August Sunday evening, but in-
doors we are gathered in the comfort of this air-conditioned, brightly
lit sacred place.[1] Tonight commences the "First Annual Finance
Convention," which will continue this entire week. Some of the
most famous names and the brightest stars of the Word of Faith
Movement—the televangelists and Faith teachers Creflo Dollar, John
Avanzini, Leroy Thompson, and Markus Bishop—are in town to
teach believers what the Bible "really" says about God's will for the
prosperity of the faithful. With the power of this message, perhaps
they will be able to convert large numbers of nonbelievers, drawing
them into the fold with the promise of the many material as well as
spiritual benefits of being saved. Throughout the week, daily and
nightly services, seminars, and workshops will be offered to eager
minds and hearts. At the center of all this activity will be faith in
God's desire to bestow financial prosperity upon Christians bold
enough to name it and claim it as their own.

    The congregation is loud and excited. They are expecting to
profit from the insights shared by the speaker, Leroy Thompson.
And he does not fail to deliver. Upon concluding his opening prayer,
he asks the congregation to continue standing and to "repeat a few

things" after him. He tells us that by having us say these things he is actually setting us up "to hear what the spirit of God is gonna say" to us tonight and throughout the week, concerning God's will for the improvement of the material condition of the life of each individual present.

The first of these "confessions," as they are called in the Word of Faith Movement, is "I'LL NEVER BE BROKE ANOTHER DAY IN MY LIFE!" which the congregation dutifully repeats, bursting into great applause and cheering. After waiting for the tide of applause to finally ebb, Thompson intones: "I AM EXPECTING *SUPERNATURAL INCREASE* THIS WEEK!" This time the congregation's response is even more enthusiastic than before. The excitement is contagious, spreading from person to person, increasing in intensity, as the applause takes longer to subside. The third confession, "I AM EXPECTING *SUPERNATURAL DEBT-CANCELLATION* THIS WEEK!" drives the congregation to frenzy and seems to usher in a different attitude among many in the audience. All around the auditorium, people's physical bearing seems to be changing—they appear to be standing taller now, ready to fight and aggressively take hold of these things they are personally claiming and confessing as theirs as part of a body of entitled believers.

True to his promise, Thompson's confessions seem to have indeed set the congregation up for all that will follow. The fertile ground of people's minds and hearts has been prepared to receive the seeds of knowledge that these "sowers" have come to sow during this week of teaching on financial prosperity—a course of study that many believe will surely yield a harvest in its season. That harvest is the financial and material prosperity God wishes to transfer from the hands of the sinner and bestow upon the righteous, that is, those bold, overcoming Christians who are unafraid to name and claim what is rightfully theirs as members of the body of Christ.

Thompson's address was only one moment in one year's finance convention at one local church. But it illustrates some of the common practices found in congregations that are part of the Word of Faith Movement. To outsiders it may seem strange that while other churches might be hosting weeklong revivals, meetings of a spiritual nature, this so-called Word church is hosting a convention for the express purpose of concentrating on what many would see as the worldly issue of money, or finances. The people here tonight want to *know more*—more about how it is squarely within God's will for them to be prosperous; more about how they can "position" themselves to be blessed financially; more about the conditions for receiving financial blessings from God; and more about what they should do with those financial blessings once they are poured out upon them. And this team of teachers is here to instruct them in these matters, with the Bible as their textbook. In a commonly invoked scriptural passage, from Hosea 4:6, God has said: "My people are destroyed for lack of knowledge." No one here tonight intends to be thus destroyed.

The Word of Faith Movement and Its Origins

The Word of Faith Movement is one of many new forms of evangelical, charismatic Christianity to develop in the United States since World War II. It is a contemporary American religious subculture made up of denominationally independent churches, ministries, Bible training colleges and other educational institutions, voluntary organizations and fellowships, information and entertainment production facilities, and mass media broadcast networks.[2] Rather than being part of a formal organizational structure, all of these entities are bound together into a relational network, based upon a shared understanding of the Bible, according to the movement's doctrine, the Faith Message.

Founders of the Movement

It has commonly been thought (by both insiders and outsiders) that the late Kenneth Erwin Hagin, Sr., was the founder of the Word of Faith Movement. Hagin has been called "the granddaddy of the Faith teachers" and was known affectionately by many in the movement as "Dad" Hagin. Some of the most prominent—and apparently most prosperous—of today's Faith teachers point to Hagin as their "spiritual father." Among these are the pastors Kenneth Copeland of Forth Worth, Texas, and Frederick K. C. Price of Los Angeles, California.[3] A prolific author, since 1966 Hagin has published and distributed a veritable mountain of books and audio tapes in which the major points of the Faith Message have been (and continue to be) explicated. In on-site bookstores at many Word of Faith Movement churches, one can usually find Hagin's books and tapes prominently displayed. In light of Hagin's high visibility throughout this subculture, it is understandable that so many would presume him to be the leader—if not the actual founder—of the movement. But upon further investigation, it becomes clear that Hagin was not the founder of the Word of Faith Movement, nor was he the principle architect of its belief system.

According to recent scholarship on the origins of the movement and its doctrine, the author of the original teachings was the independent evangelist and Bible teacher E. W. Kenyon (1867–1948), a little-known figure in American religious history. Several scholars have identified Kenyon as "the historical root from which the Faith Movement grew."[4] It appears that it was Kenyon who took a variety of ideological, philosophical, and theological influences from the period around the turn of the twentieth century and synthesized them into a body of work, albeit unsystematically formulated, that inspired what has become a worldwide phenomenon. The philosophies Kenyon drew on include: teachings of the Higher Christian Life segment of the Holiness Movement, Pentecostalism, and New Thought metaphysics (sometimes referred to as Mind Cure, Mental Healing, Mind Science, or more generally Harmonialism). Kenyon's synthesis of New Thought metaphysical philosophy, teaching that reality is actually created in the minds and affirmed in the speech of believers, gives today's Faith Message some of its most distinctive doctrinal and ritual characteristics.[5]

Hagin's teachings bore a remarkable similarity to those of Kenyon. This similarity is apparent not only in terms of concepts and doctrinal points but also in terms of the content of entire passages of text, prompting some critics to charge that Hagin plagiarized Kenyon's work. Hagin, arguing that he had arrived at his ideas and his expression of them on his own under the influence of the Holy Spirit (and that he had not met Kenyon nor even heard his teachings before Kenyon's death in 1948), adamantly denied the charge.

The connection between Kenyon and Hagin remains unclear. However, critics of the movement continue to cite Dan R. McConnell's book *A Different Gospel*, claiming that it presents conclusive evidence that Hagin plagiarized the writings of Kenyon, passing them off as his own. That those writings contained elements of New Thought (or "new age") metaphysics, which many evangelicals consider to be part of the occult and therefore Satanic, provides further evidence for these critics of the problematic origins of this movement and its teachings. According to McConnell's argument, since the basic premises of the Faith Message are "occultic," and Hagin as its recognized leader was so dishonest as to commit direct plagiarism of another minister's writings (a considerable number of pages in McConnell's book are devoted to side-by-side comparisons of texts from the two men's writings), then the movement is based on a false doctrine led by a dishonest man. McConnell's book continues to be frequently cited by critics of the Word of Faith Movement.

Hagin did establish some important organizational structures that helped lay the foundation for the development and expansion of today's movement. In 1962 he formed his church and ministry, the Kenneth E. Hagin Evangelistic Association (now known as Kenneth Hagin Ministries, Inc.). Following the establishment of his ministry, he severed his denominational affiliation with the Assemblies of God, becoming an "Independent." In 1966 Hagin moved to Tulsa, Oklahoma, where Oral Roberts, a colleague of his, had already located his own headquarters. Once in Tulsa, Hagin began broadcasting his teachings on the radio in his "Faith Seminar of the Air" (a name recalling "Kenyon's

Church of the Air"). Hagin also began publishing his teachings in *The Word of Faith* magazine (from which the name of the movement comes). Finally, to teach a new generation of ministers and prepare them to lead congregations based on these teachings, he founded the Rhema Correspondence School in 1968 and in 1974 the Rhema Bible Training Center. Since its doors opened 30 years ago, scores of new Faith teachers have graduated and begun Word of Faith ministries of their own.

Hagin's personal background is similar to that of Kenyon in several significant ways. Both Kenyon and Hagin came from less than privileged social class origins, and Hagin was chronically ill as a child. Both had limited formal education and distrusted denominational creeds and structures—particularly academically trained theologians. Both men had switched their denominational affiliations at least once in their lives, eventually becoming independent. They founded Bible training centers to pass on their teachings to new generations of church leaders, were prolific publishers, and used the mass media—radio in particular—to further their message. At the heart of the message was their promotion of a higher, "better" life that faithful Christians can experience if only they are taught to alter their thinking and be bold enough to expect more than mere spiritual blessing as a result of their salvation.

These men's experiences have left a lasting imprint on today's movement and its doctrine. For example, the movement's independence from denominational authority and administration might be traced back to the teachings of these men; voluntary associations and fellowships are the principle types of organization that structure the movement. Along with their rejection of denominational affiliation in favor of complete independence and autonomy, many in the movement have embraced their antiintellectual stance toward biblical interpretation.

The Greek word transliterated as "rhema" is frequently used among movement insiders and is defined in Thayer and Smith's *Greek Lexicon* as "that which is or has been uttered by the living voice, thing spoken, word."[6] In the Word of Faith Movement, the term is used to refer to the direct revelation of God's intents, purposes, promises, power, and very character through scripture, also referred to as the Word, and through prayer. This direct revelation of God's will and mind through his Word and prayer is seen as a purer form of knowledge and source of scriptural meaning than that which can be attained or accomplished through the intellect in formal training and study in biblical exegesis and hermeneutics. The knowledge of God's will that can be attained by common folk, those like Kenyon and Hagin, who may not be college or seminary educated, is more highly valued. According to their point of view, denomination-based educational institutions teach students to interpret the

Bible according to the denomination's core beliefs, but those interpretations are often not what the Bible "really" says, especially concerning believers' God-given right to material prosperity and other controversial issues about which they claim to have discerned the true mind of God.

As with all other parts of their doctrine, copious scriptural references are provided as "prooftexts" in support of this assertion. Certainly neither of these men nor the movement that followed them were the first to raise questions or offer insights into the complex nature of sacred textual interpretation, but the point here is simply to show how certain elements of the respective back-grounds of both Kenyon and Hagin resonate in their beliefs and teachings concerning believers' divinely appointed entitlement to material wealth and physical health as part of their earthly reward. In light of the contribution of E. W. Kenyon to today's Word of Faith Movement, it seems appropriate to characterize Hagin as the man who took Kenyon's teachings to a much broader audience than their original author was able to reach. From the middle of the twentieth century to the present Hagin played a major part in keeping the spirit of Kenyon's thought alive. It seems clear that most of the core concepts contained in today's Faith Message apparently did not come *from* Hagin, the man many people see as the movement's founder, as much as they came *through* him from E. W. Kenyon.

Core Beliefs and Practices

The Faith Message is a mélange of elements drawn and recombined anew from a variety of traditions, including Evangelicalism, neo-Pentecostalism, and, most important, New Thought metaphysics. Three basic points form the core of the Faith Message. These are: the principle of knowing who you are in Christ; the practice of positive confession (and positive mental attitude); and a world-view that emphasizes material prosperity and physical health as the divine right of every Christian.

Knowing "Who You Are in Christ"

First, knowing "who you are in Christ" is, according to those within the Word of Faith Movement, the key to living the higher Christian life that being born again will provide for all who will just accept it. In fact, abundant life has already been made available to anyone who dares to trust in the promises of God as given in the Bible and will simply *name* what they want and then *claim* it as theirs by faith. They are taught not to doubt the end result even though they don't see it—to "walk by faith and not by sight"—and to never make a *negative* confession, never let it come from their mouths that what they have asked for will not be done. All this is to be done in the authority given believers "in Jesus' name." Receiving this revelation of one's rights and privileges as a new creation in Christ is the first step to success and abundant life in this world. It is also the basis for living a life of holiness and separation from a lifestyle of sin like that of those in "the world," in order to ensure one's getting into heaven in the next life.

According to this most basic principle of the Faith Message, the Bible is actually a contract between the born-again believer and God. This notion of the contract between God and the believer has its origins in Kenyon's writing on the subject.[7] According to Kenyon and those who followed from him, that contract and its terms are spelled out in the Bible. It is this notion of rights and privileges that allows followers of this teaching to speak with a sense of entitlement to the best things that life in this present world has to offer. These benefits of being in Christ are legally guaranteed and protected by *spiritual* law. Believers are entitled to expect a better life as a result and reward for being in relationship with God through Christ. Only then can they exercise the spiritual authority that will allow them to reap those immeasurable material as well as immaterial benefits that have been laid up for them. Those who do not know who they are in Christ are often spoken of as living "beneath their privileges." Movement members are cautioned against becoming this type of believer, who may, indeed, be headed for heaven when he or she dies but is living a "defeated" life in this present world in which he or she may be suffering physically or emotionally or may be among those living under the curse of poverty.

In the Word of Faith Movement, "knowing" and renewal of the mind, habitual patterns of thought, are central to being able to appropriate, or claim as one's own, the blessings that come along with spiritual salvation. This knowledge is to be gained through direct revelation from God to the individual believer (again referred to as "rhema" in the movement) through the reading of scripture, prayer, or through the utterances of someone under the influence of the Holy Spirit (like a minister or Bible teacher). It is not necessarily gained through the sort of intellectual training one would receive in a seminary, college, or university. People who have degrees—especially if they disagree with the movement's teachings—are frequently depicted in its literature and by its ministers as having allowed their education to hinder their ability to read the Bible and to understand what God "really" means to say. Theological complexities are broken down into simple spiritual laws and principles that will work for *anyone* who is willing to apply them in faith. The knowledge of these principles has been made available to those who possess certain types of knowledge that do not come from formal training, and is usually not possessed by seminary-trained ministers (or anyone else who disagrees with movement doctrine). In various direct and indirect ways, members are taught that they "know" more than those outside of the movement. It is on the basis of their knowing—starting with knowing "who they are in Christ"—that they expect to be blessed as abundantly as they do. It is in this respect that the doctrine appears to move in the direction of Gnosticism, the belief that salvation comes through knowledge.

Positive Confession

"Name it and claim it" is a phrase that many detractors use pejoratively to describe one of the Word of Faith Movement's central practices: positive confession. Members are taught that once they know who they are in Christ, they can then speak the same words about themselves that God has spoken about them in the Bible. This allows them to access and exercise the power vested in them through their identification with Christ's finished work on the cross. According to this notion, believers can "think God's thoughts after him and speak his words after him" as well. In the biblical account of creation, God spoke and there was light. The Faith Message teaches believers that the same world-creating power is theirs as born-again Christians, and that it is a spiritual law that the spoken word sets creative (or destructive) forces in motion.

This practice of speaking only in positive confessions is one of the most readily apparent, misunderstood, and derided elements in the Word of Faith system of beliefs and practices. Members are encouraged to always be vigilant concerning the power their words carry in shaping their thinking and their subsequent lives or realities. Many in the movement frequently verbally affirm things like "I am the head and not the tail," taken from a passage in Deuteronomy in which an extensive blessing is promised to those obedient to the dictates of the Law (followed by a correspondingly extensive *curse* for the disobedient). It is not enough to reply to the question "How are you?" with "Fine." According to this teaching, one should reply with "Blessed" or "Blessed, on the top and rising" or some other such positive affirmation of one's condition. Never is one to reply "Sick" or "Struggling," lest acknowledgement of one's present condition signal acceptance of negative circumstances, which in turn signals the lack of faith that is thought to have brought one to that position in the first place (even though these responses may actually be closer to the truth).

Another example of the role of positive confession in the Word of Faith Movement can be found in their use of music. Those responsible for the music in so-called Word churches tend to be very adamant that songs used in services must not reflect the type of negative thinking and speaking that they find in the traditional songs and hymns of the mainline denominational churches from which so many of them have come (referred to by many in the movement to as "the First Church"). For example, the well-known hymn "Amazing Grace"—if sung at all—would be likely to be altered from its original "Amazing Grace, how sweet the sound / that saved a *wretch* like me" to "Amazing Grace, how sweet the sound / that saved some*one* like me." It would be acceptable, however, to sing "I once *was* lost, but *now* I'm found / *was* blind, but *now* I see" because the present condition is a positive one.

The alteration of one small word in an entire hymn might seem to an outsider insignificant. But it is based on belief in the creative power in positive and negative confession. It is seen as inappropriate to affirm something negative about oneself in any way, even in a song. Members see themselves in relation to God as having a new identity, redeemed from an old sin nature and not just "an ol', rank, sinner," as one respondent forcefully expressed it.

Not just verbal confessions but, movement members are taught, also their thoughts and self-talk are to be guarded, governed, and kept positive and "scriptural." Believers are encouraged to be diligent in maintaining a positive mental attitude and inner dialogue. Mental discipline, mental "hygiene," or self-censorship, should be an ongoing practice as demonstration of one's faith. The passage from Romans 12:1 in which the apostle Paul encourages believers to be "transformed by the renewing of [their] minds" informs this belief that spiritual transformation and regeneration comes, at least in part, from the minds and thoughts of believers being changed by accepting what the Bible teaches. As in other religions with their basis in New Thought or Mind Science, for members of the Word of Faith Movement, there is indeed power in positive thinking.

Prosperity, Divine Health, and Material Wealth

Those who teach from the Word of Faith perspective claim to know why so many faithful Christians who tithe, give offerings, and financially support ministries in other forms do not prosper financially.[8] According to one teacher, John Avanzini, such faithful people are trapped in a "lifestyle of poverty and lack" by the force of their own thoughts and ideas internalized from other, more traditional, church teachings about the proper relationship between faith and finances. Avanzini, like many others in the movement, argues that many Christians have been taught in traditional, denominational churches that Jesus was poor and that they should also be poor in order to truly identify with him. These people will never be able to receive prosperity from God until their subconscious minds have been relieved of their misconceptions about who Jesus was financially. They will have to change their way of thinking about material prosperity in order to have the kind of faith they need to receive the riches God has for them. The idea that Jesus and his disciples were not poor but had houses and a common treasury from which Judas Iscariot embezzled funds is an important part of the Word of Faith Movement's teaching on the subject. Perhaps most arresting of Avanzini's statements on the material wealth of Christ is that, from his reading of scripture, Jesus actually wore "designer" clothes and that it is God's will for believers to do so as well.

This claim is a prime illustration of today's Faith Message concerning prosperity: contemporary notions of designer clothes and other conspicuous symbols of material success are turned back and used as a lens through which to understand and to redefine God's promises to give the believer a life of abundance. According to this teaching, people may be giving money to their churches and other ministries in the form of tithes (10 percent of their *gross* income) and other offerings (regular offerings, "love offerings," building projects, missionary offerings, alms for the poor, and so on) and still be "broke." The Faith Message also teaches that the giving of monetary offerings should be thought of as sowing seeds. Oral Roberts's notion of "seed-faith" is the origin of this. Once again, using scripture as the basis, members are taught that if they sow seeds of money, they should expect to receive a harvest of money in kind. When asked why there are those who do give money to their churches in offerings and do not have the financial blessings they are told to expect, Avanzini says their own subconscious minds are keeping them from the kind of prosperity he describes and attributes to Jesus. The movement teaches that according to scripture, if God gave such great prosperity to Jesus, he would not withhold it from today's believer who is in Christ, identified with Christ, and made virtually indistinguishable from Christ in God's eyes. However, one must change his or her way of thinking concerning such matters if this level of blessing is ever to be realized.

Criticisms of the Doctrine

The Faith Message has many critics. There are those who claim that although there may actually be some "kernel" of truth located somewhere deep within, the teaching is either willfully heretical or ignorantly in error. This charge usually comes from those with formal training in biblical exegesis, who see this doctrine as yet another example of the ways the classical Christian gospel has been misinterpreted by incompetent, uneducated, albeit sometimes sincere, believers to suit their own limited understanding of it. Or it is being consciously "butchered" for financial gain by a group of educated, cynical charlatans engaged in one of the oldest rackets in history.

Some say that the message teaches an oversimplified conception of what faith is or what it is supposed to do. People are being deceived and led into thinking that all they have to do is believe or want something badly enough—and continually confess it in their speech—and then God is obligated to fulfill their wishes. In other words, the notion that humanity's purpose on earth is to serve a sovereign God has been inverted so that God has become the servant of humanity, supplying every need and responding to whim. The use of positive confession is seen by many critics as analogous to the use of magical formulas and incantations. They see this practice as tantamount to an attempt to "Christianize" practices that are best left within the realm of witchcraft and "new age" religion, both of which they consider part of the occult. Rather than believing in one's own faith as a powerful force, one should direct that faith toward God. According to this view, contemporary believers have come to trust in their own faith—and their exercise of it in practices like positive confession—more than they rely on a sovereign God alone to meet their needs (and not necessarily their desires). According to those who subscribe to this view, orthodox Christianity teaches that the believer's faith is to be focused on and in all ways refer to God through Jesus Christ. The notion of construing faith in God as a "formula for success" and then expecting the formula to work on one's behalf is for these critics an affront to some of the most basic tenets of Christian theology.

Another criticism is that with so much emphasis on the tangible, material rewards of faith, there is an implied condemnation of those who are not healthy, wealthy, and prosperous as having deficient faith or no faith at all. Those who are in some way or another suffering from sickness or even from poverty are defined as "cursed" or, worst of all, presumed to somehow be "in sin," according to the explicit as well as implicit messages contained in the doctrine. This is, perhaps, the strongest of the criticisms of the prosperity teaching.

These criticisms all point to the position that the Faith Message is yet another way contemporary evangelical Christianity has succumbed to the pressures to compete, assimilate, and accommodate itself and its conservative message to the larger, more materialistic and secular culture in which it is embedded. Instead, critics argue, believers should continue in the struggle to resist the temptation to give people what they want to hear and to offer them a truly prophetic message, designed to lead them into a more godly life and lifestyle, rather than "pandering" to their lowest impulses, as seems to be the case in so many forms of secular belief and popular cultural products.

The runaway success of the book *The Prayer of Jabez* shows how the worldview so characteristic of the Word of Faith Movement has come to resonate among contemporary Christians even outside the movement. The book and its many product tie-ins (its sequel *Fruit of the Vine*, framed art prints, journals, jewelry, more than one music CD project, and even decks of prayer cards) all expand upon and promote the contemporary relevance of an obscure biblical character's one-sentence prayer for God's blessing in the form of an enlarged territory and material increase. Their popularity serves as a pointed example for many critics of the commercialization and self-centered materialism of contemporary evangelical Christianity. The Word of Faith Movement and its promises of exorbitant levels of material wealth and success for the faithful is frequently cited as having prepared fertile ground for this continued assimilation of Christianity to the dictates of the larger, secular world that the church is supposed to be "in but not of."[9]

Structure and Distribution of the Word of Faith Movement

Organizationally, after several decades of existence the Word of Faith is still best described as a movement and not a denomination. It is a relational community of believers, voluntary organizations, fellowships, conferences, and ministries loosely bound by a shared doctrine, a network without a definite leader or governing body. Because it is not a denomination and has no centralized, governing body or hierarchical structure, it is difficult to map this bit of religious territory against the larger contours of contemporary American religious experience. Increasingly, elements of the Faith Message are finding their way into the teachings of denominational churches that might not consider themselves part of the movement. We might find adherents (of parts or all) of this teaching among those identifying themselves as "evangelicals," "charismatics," "Pentecostals," "nondenominationals," or just "Christians" on traditional surveys of religious identification or affiliation.

Four main organizations provide primary structure for the meeting and interaction of ministers and their ministries, for the distribution and dissemination of the message, and the training of new generations of Faith teachers.

1973: Trinity Broadcast Network

Trinity Broadcast Network (TBN) bills itself as "The Largest Christian [television] Network in the World."[10] From the looks of its distribution, they are probably correct in this assessment. The network was founded in 1973 by Paul and Jan Crouch in association with Jim and Tammy Faye Bakker, the husband-and-wife televangelist team who were disgraced in the late 1980s when reports of their legendary financial excesses became public. Headquartered in Santa Ana, California, today TBN claims that it owns and is affiliated with 536 networks in North and South America. The network's programming is carried in at least sixty-two countries, in the Caribbean and Pacific, on the African continent, and in Europe (including the former Soviet Union). The network also broadcasts its programming via thousands of cable carriers throughout the world, reaching private properties like residential trailer parks and apartment complexes. Even a prison in Arizona serves as a cable outlet where viewers are still within reach of TBN and the Faith Message.

At its International Production Center in Irving, Texas, TBN programming is translated into various languages and prepared for broadcast around the world. The flagship production, *Praise the Lord* (PTL), which is broadcast live from several facilities in the United States, is a "born again" variety show; many Christian celebrities (and some celebrities who also happen to be Christians) appear on the show. These guests frequently include well-known pastors—especially those from within the Word of Faith Movement—who lead enormous, "mega," churches or ministries. The network also produces original Christian programs, including gospel music concerts, live coverage of major Christian events, health and fitness programs from a Christian perspective, children's programs, contemporary Christian music videos, holiday specials, marriage enrichment series, Christian dramas and television movies, and regular worship services from some of this country's largest churches. The network also produces major motion pictures (or has acted as partner in their production).

A satellite network, TBN Latino, will soon cover Central and South America with Spanish-language programming. The "Good News" network, TBN Latino is slated to service the whole country of Brazil with Portuguese-language programming, and there are already broadcasts via satellite and from overseas studios to various cities and regions of Europe, Africa, and other parts of the world.[11]

1979: International Convention of Faith Ministries

The International Convention of Faith Ministries (ICFM) was founded in 1979 by the late Reverend Doyle "Buddy" Harrison (son-in-law of Kenneth Hagin, Sr.) as a voluntary organization for licensed, ordained ministers who are committed to "holding forth, contending for, and propagating the word of faith worldwide."[12] The ICFM's headquarters are located in Arlington, Texas. An international organization, ICFM also has offices and directors placed in a number of nations and elsewhere in the United States. It holds regular conventions during which ministers come together for fellowship, training, and inspiration before returning to the care of their respective flocks.

A voluntary organization, ICFM is a fellowship whose membership is restricted to self-identified ministers.[13] As a voluntary organization, it does not exercise regulatory authority over its members. Rather, the purpose of ICFM is to provide a setting for ministers to interact and offer mutual support. In the United States, the membership of ICFM is distributed throughout 298 cities, with a combined total number of 377 ministries in 41 states. These ministries may or may not be churches, and the majority of them (65 percent) can be found in Southern states. The states with the largest overall numbers of ICFM members and ministries include: Texas, with 59 ministries in 36 cities; Florida, with 33 ministries in 23 cities; and Missouri, with 32 ministries in 26 cities. Internationally, ICFM's members are distributed throughout 23 countries, with a total of 236 ministries in 159 locations.

1985: The Rhema Ministerial Alliance International

Founded in 1985 by Kenneth Hagin, Sr., the Rhema Ministerial Association International (RMAI) is the third of the four organizations that structure the Word of Faith Movement. A part of Kenneth Hagin Ministries, RMAI is another important medium for the perpetuation and dissemination of the Faith Message into successive generations of Faith teachers and ministers. Similar to ICFM, the RMAI is an organization providing support and fellowship for its members who are also ordained ministers. The difference is that the members are generally graduates of Hagin's Rhema Bible Training Center, who are licensed and/or ordained by the organization.

The number of churches with RMAI members as their leaders is published annually in the form of an RMAI directory in The Word of Faith magazine. According to figures reported in 2001, RMAI boasts a membership of 1,315 churches pastored by Rhema graduates in 1,123 cities throughout the United States. As is the case with ICFM, the concentration of these member or affiliated churches is overwhelmingly Southern, with almost half (48 percent) of member churches located in states like Texas (79 churches in 72 cities); Florida (79 churches in 60 cities); Oklahoma (70 churches in 46 cities); and Missouri (61 churches in 53 cities). Outside of the South, California has the highest overall number of RMAI member or affiliate churches in the country, with 85 churches in 77 cities.

Internationally, the 2001 directory reported 140 RMAI member (or affiliated) churches distributed throughout 133 cities in 52 nations. Outside of the continental United States, Canada has the largest number of RMAI member churches, with 18 throughout its provinces. There is surprisingly little overlap between the names of ICFM member churches and ministries and those pastored by RMAI members. In total, the number of ministries or churches led or pastored by members of either the ICFM or the RMAI is 1,692 in the United States and 376 overseas in more than 60 countries.

1990: Fellowship of Inner-City Word of Faith Ministries

With its headquarters at Crenshaw Christian Center in South Central Los Angeles, the Fellowship of Inner-City Word of Faith Ministries (FICWFM) is another voluntary organization for ministers who share a common relationship to the Faith Message.[14] Founded in August 1990, its mission is to provide support and service to churches located in inner cities in the United States and abroad. The organization's mission statement explicitly says that "although FICWFM serves as a 'spiritual covering' for its member-pastors and members, it does not govern any of its member-ministries—each ministry operates personally, privately and independently of FICWFM—the member-ministry has no reporting responsibility to FICWFM."[16] The organization's by-laws and a 24-member board of directors, with Dr. Frederick K. C. Price as president, govern the fellowship.

Across the country, annual conferences of member congregations are held in each of FICWFM's eight national regions. The fellowship also hosts an annual convention each summer at its national headquarters, Crenshaw Christian Center in South Central Los Angeles, during which featured speakers teach on various aspects of Christian life from the Word of Faith Movement perspective, business meetings are convened, and other organizational business is attended to. Although FICWFM is an organization for ministers, individual members of the congregations led by them also become members and are welcomed and included as participants at the convention. These annual conventions also include activities for the attending congregations' members, as well as special programs for the youth and children.

The membership of FICWFM is distributed throughout 35 states in America and 3 foreign countries, with a membership of approximately 300 pastors or ministers, representing a combined congregational membership of approximately 150,000 believers in the churches over which these pastors or ministers preside.[15] The dynamic nature of religious phenomena in general (and particularly movements like the Word of Faith that do not have formal organizational structures to gather and disseminate such information) makes it difficult to draw conclusions about the actual number of churches, ministers, and followers who are part of the movement. But from membership figures of the movement's core organizations, we can estimate that the Word of Faith Movement consists of between 2,300–2,500 churches, ministries, fellowships, or television networks in the United States and in more than 60 countries abroad.

The Scope of This Book

This book looks at the Word of Faith Movement in the context of contemporary American religion in general but also as a distinct subculture in its own right. It has been written in the hope of educating those outside of the movement (as well as insiders) by situating this specific region on the map of contemporary American religion in a historical context, in a congregational context, and in the context of individuals' daily lives. The Word of Faith Movement shares many characteristics with other religious movements that have received considerably more media and research attention in the academic and popular presses.

The majority of existing research on contemporary American religion, especially with respect to the megachurches, tends to focus on movements and congregations with a predominately white, middle-class, suburban membership base. Moreover, although some of these movements do have large numbers of African American members, little attention is given to the differences in meaning that derive from the central role that religion, particularly Christianity and the Black Church, has played in the formation and maintenance of a self-sustaining Black community from early on in the experience of African enslavement in the Americas to the present.

The specificity of African American adaptation of traditional African religions and Euro-American Christianity has not been adequately considered in many books dealing with contemporary religious movements with large numbers of African American followers. The contemporary African American religious experience continues to be underresearched and only partially understood in terms of all the contours, nuances, and overall complexity of evangelical religious thought, practice, and, most important, change and continuity at the present juncture in Western history. A distinctive element of this book is its emphasis on the inner workings and the congregational culture of a Word of Faith Movement church led by an African American pastor, with a predominately African American membership and worship style, and situated in an urban setting in a neighborhood with a substantial African American presence.

This book is derived from a study utilizing participant observation and in-depth interviews with a small subset of members of a large Word of Faith Movement congregation in Sacramento, California. Rather than focusing on the insights and perspectives of religious leaders and others who have a regular venue or platform from which to communicate their understandings of doctrine, the focus here is on the people who make up this movement—"the people in the pews." The goal is to allow them to speak about what they make of the movement's doctrine and how they struggle to make sense of and apply it in their own daily lives. In addition to innumerable conversations and informal interviews with family, friends, colleagues, and acquaintances all familiar with the movement and the local congregation that was the principal setting for this study's fieldwork, formal interviews were conducted with 20 people, 19 of whom were current or past members of the Word of Faith Movement.

For large numbers of believers in the United States and in a host of nations abroad, the belief that it is God's will for them to be healthy and wealthy and to enjoy all the best this present world has to offer before they die and go to heaven serves as the core of their understanding of their relationship to the sacred. In this book you will have the chance to hear from some of these "everyday theologians," who speak in their own language and from their own perspective about what they believe and how they try to practice it in their daily lives. Using personal narratives, in which individuals recount their experiences as members of a particular Word of Faith Movement congregation, this study presents a portrait of some of the *creativity* that can be found in everyday, vernacular forms of religious belief and practice. It also illustrates some of the ways in which individuals struggle to make sense of profound, complex, and frequently confusing doctrine. They do so in the interstices between the "shoulds" invoked by religious establishments and the "musts" that represent the ways things actually are as experienced in their everyday lives. People of any given faith, denomination, local congregation, or even household do not all hear doctrine in the same way. This book's goal is to illustrate some of the dynamism and energy inherent in the ongoing process of negotiation that characterizes the construction of meaning out of religious doctrine.

I

Bearing Witness

Be ready always to give an answer to every man that asketh you a
reason of the hope that is in you.

—1 Peter 3:15

To understand the "real" meaning of the Word of Faith Movement,
we need to inquire of those for whom it serves as an important part
of their experience with and expression of the sacred. This chapter
focuses on some of the lay people, or the audience, of the Faith
Message. Here these everyday theologians articulate their particular
understandings of the movement and its creed. They also discuss
how they came to adopt the Faith Message—its principles, beliefs,
and practices—as their own and how they understand its meanings
against the horizon of other forms of religion they knew before embracing this one.

The Members Speak

The experiences of three respondents have been singled out. These
individuals' stories seemed to highlight and express most vividly
some of the dominant themes to emerge in talking to people about
so personal and intimate a topic as their faith. Their accounts of
their personal experiences and insights demonstrate that the understanding and meaning of religion as it is lived in everyday contexts

can be quite nuanced and complicated, and often fraught with difficulty. Their stories help bring abstract points of doctrine into the realm of the concrete and the real. Please allow me to introduce them.

"Cassandra" is an African American woman in her mid-30s. At the time of our interview she was single, was college-educated, held a master's degree in social work (MSW), and had a career as a social worker at the Sacramento County Child Protective Services. Her perspectives on the movement and how her own understanding and application of the doctrine have shaped her life experiences are well expressed in her comments and the experiences she relates. "Russell," a married Baby Boomer, was just about to celebrate his fiftieth birthday when we met. Although he was raised in a Jewish household, he has been with the Word of Faith Movement since its early days in the late 1970s and continues to be active in his local church today. Russell is a blue-collar worker who offers an example of some of the distinctive and interesting ways that religion is given meaning in the lives of those who hear and use it. "Katia" is a single, 25-year-old immigrant from Ukraine. At the time of our first meeting she was a student at California State University at Sacramento. Since her family's arrival in the United States when she was a teenager, fleeing religious persecution for being Evangelicals, she has become an upwardly mobile, *new* young American woman with an interesting perspective on the Word of Faith Movement and its message. In addition to these three, the experiences of several other respondents provide even more insight into the ways in which various individuals grapple with complex theological concepts and teachings in the context of their everyday lives.

Cassandra: "I felt like I was no longer put in a box"

I have known her for many years, and the first part of our meeting (as well as the phone call made to schedule it) centered on catching up on all that had taken place in both of our lives since last we talked. Cassandra is an extroverted, gregarious person with a great sense of humor. Because these memories crystallize the image I have carried in my mind of her and her personality, I wanted to get her take on this topic. I expected that she would not hold back in terms of what she thought, and I was not disappointed.

I remembered seeing her years ago play the role of a demon in a church-sponsored Easter play. She really seemed to relish the part (as did some of the others) because she got the chance to be "evil" in a play at church. But along with all the fun and her image of being very gregarious and outgoing, I also remembered over the years that along with her great depth of humor, there seemed to be a very serious side to Cassandra. At various times when I would run into her, we would both discuss our respective progress through the labyrinth of our educational programs. She was attending the local state university and was several years ahead of me while I was still at the local community college. I also remember learning that her brother—her only sibling—had been killed. He had been shot to death in Oakland, their hometown, in a drive-by shooting. Obviously, Cassandra had been greatly affected by his untimely death, and there was a great depth of sadness about her whenever she spoke of him. The violence of the inner city, from which she had come but also had managed to escape by relocating to pursue her education, had claimed her only brother. In the time since this tragedy, she had completed her MSW degree and become a social worker, protecting and rescuing children.

When we met for the first time to do these interviews, it was at the coffee shop located in the Downtown Galleria in Sacramento, a complex of shops and businesses, which had been the site of an all-day training session that she had been required to attend as part of her job. I waited several minutes past our scheduled meeting time until she descended in the glass elevator from above, at the conclusion of the class and after talking with some of her colleagues. I could hear them chatting and laughing as I sat at a table below, nervously checking my recorder and rehearsing my questions, so I would sound more professional and less like a nervous graduate student. One of the first things I noticed about her was that she had lost a bit of weight since I had last seen her. She was walking with a crutch, having recently undergone surgery on her knee.

When we met, we embraced. She seemed to me to have grown up and matured a great deal since I had last seen her many years ago. But as we talked, the "old" Cassandra came bursting through again. One of the things I had always liked about her was her down-to-earth persona. She was more than just someone who was a Christian with no other interests outside those circumscribed and approved by the church. Like many others in this demanding, dynamic congregation, Cassandra struggles to maintain a life separate from the dictates of the ministry while still participating in its functioning.

At the end of that first meeting, we walked out to our cars and discovered that we drove the same make and relatively late model of car. We agreed that we deserved these tangible fruits of all the labor we had both put toward gaining an education and making a life for our families and ourselves. We laughed, sharing the understanding that there was nothing at all wrong with being prosperous because we had worked hard for what we now possess. Yes, we had both moved upward since first meeting so many years before. In fact, I was quite impressed when she mentioned that she had recently taken up golf, because she was the first African American that I knew personally who played the sport. (This was, of course, before Tiger Woods became a household name.) She talked at length about how, as an African American, she did not feel that she should be limited from doing *any* type of activity simply because traditionally there have been few of "us" moving in those circles. I saw that she had indeed grown and changed tremendously since we last interacted so many years before. She had grown even beyond the expansive image of her that I had held for more than 10 years.

Having come to Faith Christian Center in 1985, Cassandra has been with the ministry and the Word of Faith Movement for many years now. She has seen many changes, from the sheer size of the ministry to the way things are done and the types of rituals allowed into the worship services. When she was first invited to visit the church by a relative, she had no idea that there even existed any such thing as a "Faith Movement" or that the church she was about to visit might be classified as part of it. In her account she explains what specific elements she would look for that would allow her to recognize the Faith Message were she to encounter a minister or someone else in a church, on television, radio, in a book, or elsewhere.

Interestingly, she (like the other respondents) described the Faith Message almost entirely in terms of what it was *not*—that is, she made sense of her present religious beliefs first in relation to the understanding and experience of Christianity she had before being introduced to the doctrine of this particular movement. I posed to her a hypothetical scenario in which she turned on the television and saw a minister speaking ("preaching" or "teaching"). I asked her to describe, based upon what she saw and heard, how she would discern whether what she was hearing was (or was not) the doctrine of the Word of Faith Movement. What were the specific cues that would allow her to recognize whether some form of doctrine was (or was not) within the symbolic, ideological, and practical parameters she used to conceptualize the Word of Faith Movement and its message? She responded:

> I think the first thing I would look at is whether it's a hell-and-
> brimstone-type message or whether it's more of a positive thinking
> [message]. I think, for *me*, the Faith movement represents more of
> your positive thinking. More of you can have what you believe you
> can have, you can have what you think you can have. Your thoughts
> determine your destiny. And if we're thinking along the lines of how
> God describes us, if we keep that in mind, we can have whatever we
> want. Within the realm of what God wants for us. So I'm looking
> for that positive [emphasis]—or that's what I see first.

When asked to explain what she thought differentiated the Faith Message from the religious background she had prior to joining Faith Christian Center in 1985, she responded:

I think the difference was what I *felt*. I felt personally more empowered to bring about the changes I wanted in my life. I wasn't just someone standing by waiting for God to bestow some sort of . . . blessing, or privilege, on me. That's what the difference was. I mean, I came out of a—I went to a Methodist church as a child—but not because of my parents, but because my best friend's father was a Methodist minister, and so I went to church with them on Sundays. So even then I wasn't looking for any particular denomination, church was just church to me. But as I compare that to the church I attend now, that was the big difference: I feel like I have more control over what happens in my life, you know? I can look at the scriptures and I can find scriptures within the Bible and know that there are things that I can create for myself. I mean, they're there, but bringing those into manifestation . . . Like how that scripture says, "speak those things that be not as though they were"— well, I didn't hear that back then. You know, I was just this somebody who was—like I said—waiting for God to finally get to my number to give me a blessing—and that's very different. I feel like I'm more in control. I have more of an active part in what happens to me in terms of my Christianity, that's it.

I was also interested in hearing which aspects of all she had seen and, most important, heard at Faith Christian Center she thought had convinced her to stay with the church and, in effect, become a member of what she later learned was the Word of Faith Movement. What about the teaching (or the church where she had heard it) convinced her to switch from the Methodist church to become a member in a nondenominational church/religious movement? She explained:

For me, as an African American woman, I felt like I was no longer put in a box. You know, I didn't have to do things because I was African American. Or, I was not limited simply because I was African American. I was a child of God first who happened to be African American. And that broadened my knowledge base, it broadened my desires. I didn't feel limited anymore; I didn't feel limited by the color of my skin. I shouldn't say simply by the color of my skin, but by people's stereotypical views of me as a African American woman. I was no longer concerned with the images that other people had about me. Because I now knew how God thought of me, and that was more important than anything. And so, I think that was the key thing, for me, that kept me there. I wasn't in this "what The Man does to you," you know, The White Man—it wasn't about that. It was about my relationship with God and what God has promised me, and me saying I'm going to live those promises. So it was getting me out of that box, that limited thinking.

Cassandra's account allows us to observe several things about the subculture of the Word of Faith Movement. First, she offers an example of the way many people in the movement speak of the teachings of the denominational churches they once attended. Cassandra admitted that her experience with the Methodist church as a child was limited. However, she notes that the Faith Message impressed her by the absence of punitive, fear-inducing "fire-and-brimstone," other-worldly kinds of sermons and the presence of a teaching that emphasized positive thinking, success, and fulfillment in this present world. This emphasis reflects the present-worldly orientation of the Faith Movement. For some people the former type of message seems to be centered on the next world and on where and how believers thought they might spend eternity.

Cassandra also singles out the theme of empowerment she hears expressed in the Faith Message. A message like this is particularly salient for those who have traditionally not had access to power, to control over their own destinies. They may have been on the lower rungs of a society's ladder, be it in terms of race, class, gender, or ethnic background. In her description and explanation of what the Faith Message means to her, she claims to have personal power and control over the circumstances of her own life. Words like "power" and "control" appear in her comments frequently.

Cassandra spoke of feeling as though, undergirded by this empowering message, she had the ability to effect the *changes* that she wanted in her own life, rather than simply having to wait helplessly and passively, however sincerely and prayerfully, for God to do something on her behalf. The notion that individuals can and should apply the scriptures instrumentally and attempt to "live the promises" in them as a tool to reconstruct their lives and situations as they would have them be is a very important part of the teaching in Word of Faith Movement churches. Cassandra's statement reveals that for her there is a sense of agency in the way she goes about her life as a Christian who is "in the world but not of it," meaning that she is not necessarily subject to the same kinds of forces and processes that others in the world may face—those without the kind of knowledge and its accompanying sense of power that comes from this body of teaching.

This is quite a different Christian identity from that which emerges out of a more traditional Christian message. The phrase "not having to wait for God to finally get to my number" is particularly expressive of this actively engaged, empowered attitude. Cassandra is a college-educated professional who has a greater number of resources available to her than some other Black women, so her comments must be placed in that context. Nevertheless, her understanding and application of the teachings of the Faith Message and its emphasis on personal empowerment allowed her to work toward the fulfillment of her dreams and goals. That is the interaction of her belief and application of the Faith Message and her experiences as a professional have provided her with the kind of lifestyle she has and the ability to make the types of claims she does. She speaks of broadening her knowledge and desires—beyond the constraints of race, class, and gender. For Cassandra as an African American, a woman, and a person from inner-city and working-class origins, the Faith Message appears to be most of all an ideology that enables her to dream larger dreams for herself than her social location would readily suggest.

"Put in a box" was an interesting way for Cassandra to express the sense of being constrained by her ascribed status as an African American woman from inner-city, working-class origins. Not resigned to accept the world and her place in it as it was first presented to her, Cassandra now finds that such images and stereotypes have been replaced in her mind by what she says God thinks about her as she reads it in the Bible. She says that she is going to live the promises of God rather than the limitations imposed upon her by her social location. The box she spoke of was a metaphor for the limited thinking from which the movement offers to help people gain freedom. She seems to be relating, from her experience and understanding of it, the Faith Message teaching that through the power of the mind, people can realize those big dreams and goals that they may have thought were beyond their reach.

The positive thinking, the sense of personal power and of *agency* to bring about and realize the biggest, most unlimited goals—"within the realm of what God wants" for her—are what Cassandra understands as being different from the Christianity she knew and understood as taught by the Methodist church of her childhood. Virtually all of the interviewees said, either directly or indirectly, that they wanted something more than what they were getting in their previous churches or than what their previous understanding of Christianity gave them. They did not say something "different," they all said something "more." When they heard the message emphasizing prosperity, self-development and self-actualization, personal power, and control over the circumstances of one's own life—and that all these things could be theirs as a result of being saved—they each realized that they had found what they'd been looking for. This theme is one of the most common and resonant of all the respondents' accounts of what the Faith Message means to them and why they accepted it.

Russell: "A lot of teachings in a lot of churches that are not Word of Faith are not real practical"

Approaching the house, I noticed that just to the right of the front door was a sign proclaiming "As for me and my house, we will serve the Lord," and I recognized a scriptural passage taken from Joshua 24:15. The sign out front and its profession—or confession, in Word of Faith Movement terms—served as the front line of this family's public practice of their faith. They were in effect "witnessing" as evangelical Christians, declaring their faith to all who would approach or enter this home.

Although I had seen him in services and church-related functions for many years, I had never met Russell until the bright November morning I showed up at his house for the interview appointment. I arrived early for our 9 a.m. appointment and knocked on the door. No one was home, so I returned to my car to wait. After a few minutes had passed, I began writing a note to leave on the door in case he had forgotten about our meeting. As I was heading back up the walk, Russell zoomed around the corner in a compact car, waving to me and smiling broadly as he continued the car's wide arc into his driveway. When he got out of the car, we shook hands, and he said he had just gone out to run a quick errand and had come back immediately because he had given his word that he would do this interview with me this morning.

Following him into the foyer of the house, I was struck by what I saw: on the wall directly across from the front door was an 8 × 10 photograph of the pastor of Faith Christian Center and his wife, taken at some recent church event. I saw this picture before I saw any photos of Russell, his wife, or any of their own family members. The prominent placement of that photograph, right at the front entrance to the house, made a strong first impression on me. To be honest, it shaped my expectations of what I would hear from him that morning. Later, during the course of our introductions and mutual self-disclosures—our attempts at getting to know each other a bit before getting down to business—he mentioned that he was 49, "the same age as Pastor," and seemed to be particularly proud of that fact. Looking around, I noticed and commented on the fact that the house had many arts and crafts objects of a religious nature, to which he responded that his wife had made several of them.

Although I was keenly aware of my limited time that morning, needing to conduct the interview and get to campus in time to teach my class, I followed Russell about as he changed his shoes and showed me around the house, explaining the significance of various objects as we went. At one point we went down the hall to the laundry room, where his Dalmatian, "Lucy," was barking and whining for attention. He commanded the dog to get into her box and even showed me one of her tricks, holding a large, bone-shaped dog biscuit on her nose and then tossing it in the air on his cue and catching it. I was impressed and commented that my new dog didn't even come when called yet. He talked about "speaking over" the dog as part of the process he had used in training her: he was using positive confession in training her, telling her she was a blessing and that she was smart and also obedient. He also spoke about her as such to me. He explained that you have to "speak positive things over your dog" if you want it to do what you want it to do.

During the course of our interview, which took place at the kitchen table, Russell told me about his wife's work in the church and the appreciation party recently given for her by some other members of the ministry. (At one point he even had me come into the living room to watch part of the videotape of the event.) He also got up in the middle of answering one of my questions and retrieved his Bible to *show* me certain scriptures to which he was referring. Although I thought it a bit strange and even eccentric at the time that he felt the need to *show* me scriptural references as we talked—after all, these were commonly used passages, and I was a member of the same church and was also quite familiar with them—Russell's actions illustrate an important part of the Word of Faith Movement culture, especially at Faith Christian Center. With so much emphasis on teaching (as opposed to preaching) and knowing (instead of feeling), people take pleasure in demonstrating their proficiency with the Bible and scripture memorization. The value placed upon spiritual display in interaction with others by quoting—or "confessing"—scripture is so great that one interviewee (whom I met with three different times) repeatedly apologized to me for not being able to recite passages verbatim as we talked. He said he was praying for God to help him get better at memorizing and reciting scriptures. Trying to reassure him, I told him not to worry about it, that I can't remember them all either, but he seemed to take this very seriously as some sort of lapse or shortcoming in his spiritual life and appeared to be quite uncomfortable and embarrassed.

One of the church's running jokes is that people in the congregation seize the slightest opportunity to "preach" whenever they get their hands on the microphone in the service or when certain members have the rare opportunity to pray aloud before the congregation at offering time or some other such point in the service. Frequently they will string together scripture after scripture in what turns out to be a very long prayer. They are taught that this is the correct way to "pray the Word." The pastor maintains guarded control over who will be given access to the pulpit and who is allowed to address the congregation. This is especially true when it comes to other ministers or to individuals who would "pray over" or "speak over" his people, the "sheep." Given the belief in the power of the spoken word to produce real, objective effects in the life of the hearer (as well as the speaker), not just anyone can stand before the congregation. When some individuals do get the chance, they try to make the most of it.

Another aspect of this culture in which there is so much stress on studying and knowing the Bible—being lay Bible scholars—was expressed when I commented on how nice his Bible was and asked if it was new (since he had actually brought it to the kitchen table in its original box). He quickly replied, "Oh, no, we just keep it in the box." In so-called Word churches like Faith Christian Center, a well-worn, even ragged Bible, marked throughout with pens, highlighting markers, and with its covers falling off signified that the owner used it regularly and was assumed to be very spiritual. By the same token, the newer a Bible looked (especially if it really were not actually new), the stronger the assumption that the person rarely used it and was less spiritual. Russell's quick response might have meant that he had taken my comment as meaning the Bible was too nice and clean to be have been used regularly.

That morning I learned many things about Russell's life and how he came to be part of the Word of Faith Movement. Raised in a Jewish household, he was "born again" as an evangelical Christian in 1978 (the year he turned 29) and began attending an Assemblies of God (Pentecostal) church. During the same week as his conversion, he attended a seminar in San Francisco led by Kenneth Hagin, Sr. He had known about Kenneth Hagin and Kenneth Copeland, another important Word of Faith Movement teacher, prior to this weekend seminar. His older brother had purchased many of their books and tapes and had attempted to share some insights from them with Russell. His brother's attempts to evangelize and introduce him to the Faith Message had met with great resistance because Russell saw his brother as "saying one thing and living another," as he related the story to me. As he remembered it, Russell didn't see any "fruit" that this particular message was having too great an effect on his brother's life—why, then, should he get excited over it? Because he saw no consistency in his brother's Christian walk, he had a difficult time accepting his witness of the Faith Message.

Russell said that before his conversion to Christianity (from his nonreligious period as a young adult), he'd been very resistant to going to church or getting saved—he had a job, paid his taxes, and voted—and, as he related it to me, "what I was doing on *my* time, to *my* body, with *my* friends, was *my* business." He also seemed to have had a fatalistic attitude toward God. He said that from his Jewish upbringing his perspective was that "God was who he was, and we did what we were supposed to do, and if it all worked out, it worked out." But after that fateful weekend of seminars, and direct exposure to the charismatic personality and the teachings of Kenneth Hagin, Russell purchased an entire tape series entitled "What Is Faith?" It was May 1978, and this was the beginning of his exposure to the Faith Message and the movement based upon it.

Over the next few years, Russell met and married his wife, Joan (on Christmas Eve, 1980), and moved to southern California as a result of a job transfer. They had continued to attend denominational churches before their move, Assemblies of God and also Foursquare, but once they were in southern California they found a new church, one that was a "Word Church." The pastor at this new church, whose name Russell declined to disclose, had been on the board of directors of one prominent Word of Faith Movement organization, as well as having been the head usher for yet another large, well-known Movement ministry. From 1982 to 1988 Russell and his wife were members of this church, as well as being active in the Full Gospel Businessmen's Association, an important organization in the formation and development of the contemporary Charismatic movement. In 1988 they moved to Sacramento, where they became members of Faith Christian Center, and have there been ever since. They have both been familiar with the Word of Faith Movement (having "cut their teeth" on it, as Russell expressed it), since they were "new babes in Christ" in the late 1970s and early 80s.

I asked Russell to reflect back on those seminars with Hagin and Copeland and to describe for me how what he first heard in the Faith Message differed from what he'd understood Christianity to be prior to his exposure to it. He answered:

> The basic difference is—it's true today more than ever before—your
> sermons were topics. Your sermons were teachings and it was, it
> was a teaching of victory. It was a teaching on how to win. It was a
> teaching based on scripture. It wasn't any "What did man think?"
> throw a sermon together without a scripture to back it up. It was a
> teaching from the Word of God that was based on how to live, how
> to win, how to be victorious in every area of your life. It didn't mat-

ter if you were dealing with how to have a relationship with a fellow employee, how to have a relationship with your wife, how to have a relationship with members of the body [all believers as the "body" of Christ]. How to deal with and understand who the Enemy [Satan] is. And so it was a very Bible-based . . . it was practical. And what I've found today is that a lot of teachings in a lot of churches that are not Word of Faith are not real practical. That a lot of pastors will gear a message to what the congregation wants to hear and not what God is saying. It's very practical and it's easy to understand, but by the same token that teaching is also gonna cause you to—once you've heard it—have to live it because [of] its accountability factor that you might not have in other churches, other pastors, other denominations.

I had never heard the term "accountability factor" used in this context before. He went on to clarify and expound upon it further:

The accountability factor is that once you've heard the Word of God, the Bible says, "To him who knows to do right and doeth it not, to him it is sin." The Bible says once you've heard, then you're responsible for it. And if you've never heard that way of life, what the Bible teaches, if you've never heard what the Bible teaches as far as submission to a pastor, to authority on your job, if wives don't care about obedience to her husband—but obedience to the Word of God first—then . . . a lot of people don't know what the Bible says because they haven't studied it themselves.

Russell's articulation of his own understanding of the Faith Message offers a glimpse into a few more of the characteristics of the culture informed by it. First, in his description of what he sees as essential to the message, he specifically mentions the emphasis on the practical application of biblical principles and spiritual "laws," the apprehension of which is the very foundation of the doctrine. According to his understanding of it, *the Faith Message is applied Christianity* in almost a scientific sense. It is taught, learned, and understood expressly to be used instrumentally as well as expressively. It is not primarily a religion of contemplation or meditation but is centered on understanding how God and the spiritual world "works" in order to live in such a way as to please him, and also so that one can be blessed by him. It assumes as given what other groups might emphasize: that Christians are in pursuit of and practicing a lifestyle of holiness and conformity to the will and dictates of God's law revealed through Christ, and concentrates on the tangible rewards of that life-style.

Second, Russell's invocation of what he called the built-in "accountability factor" is based on the premise that once believers *know* the principles and understand the commands of God they should set about applying them. Again, this is not a contemplative religious system. It is not about "getting in tune with the Universe" for the purpose of having "mere" inner peace (although that condition is part of what they would describe as "spiritual prosperity"). It is about taking that knowledge and information and realizing the power behind it in practical ways. In its insistence on the practical application of scripture, the Faith Message is very much about the acquisition and manipulation of power—supernatural power in the natural realm of human existence. It is about taking direct, aggressive action. Christians who know who they are become channels for the working out of God's supernatural power in the natural realm. When speaking of people not knowing what the Bible really says on certain issues concerning proper behavior, Russell is suggesting that people who do not know are unable to implement those teachings, thus creating the need for churches like those in the Word of Faith Movement that actually teach the people what they need to know in order to live "correctly."

Katia: "My parents could not understand why in the world would I go to 'the Black people's' church'"

I met Katia and her friend Mila at a small cafe owned and operated by the church. It was my first visit there, although at the end of each of the services on Sunday morning, the day's lunch menu and specials are read just before the benediction and the dismissal of the congregation. All in attendance are encouraged to go there for food, coffee or tea, and, of course, fellowship. Lending their patronage to the church's cafe by eating there after services is a way for members to "reinvest" their money in the ministry, instead of flocking to one of the other nearby coffee shops or restaurants often frequented by the "after-church crowd." Lining the walls all around the triangle-shaped room were a number of framed posters and old newspaper clippings with the pastor as the subject. The restaurant's name, Fancy's, came from the nickname the pastor had used in his younger days when he had been an amateur boxer.

The cafe is located about two blocks from the church and is staffed by church members. This particular August evening, the television set was blaring in one corner of the cafe, with an action drama of some sort playing on it.

Working as the server was an African American woman, a graduate of the Overcomers' program, the residential substance abuse rehabilitation ministry run by the church. She arrived at the table to take our order: "just" three coffees, as she repeated it. (After watching me talking and listening intently to two women for the better part of an hour, as I was leaving she asked me what I was selling.) Aside from the child who was with the server, Katia, Mila, and I were the only people in the cafe this evening. Since it was the first meeting for all three of us—and because they were two young women—I had thought it best to meet them at a public place near the church.

With the heat and with the television blaring inside, I decided it might be better to take our coffees outside to sit at one of the sidewalk tables with um-brellas. I needed to be able to tape-record our conversation, but the noise level was even worse out there, with buses, cars, and 18-wheelers constantly passing. Much of this background noise and "local color" is captured on the tape. In fact, there is even a point at which an apparently homeless woman's voice is heard on the tape as she approaches us asking for some change for food, which is not unusual for the neighborhood where this church is teaching and spend-ing so much time talking about prosperity. A paradox, perhaps, but it could also be said that teaching about prosperity is needed. I gave her some change, and she was on her way.

In the course of our conversation that evening, I learned that Katia had come to the United States recently from Ukraine, part of the former Soviet Union. Her story is a fascinating one. She came to this country as one of many religious refugees. Especially interesting is Katia's description of her thoughts and beliefs concerning Black people before she left Ukraine and how they have changed since coming to the United States, where she belongs to a predomi-nately African American congregation. She tells of how the "welcoming" ritual in the church made her feel comfortable and helped her determine that this was a ministry that she would like to be a part of. But she also says that many of the older generation cannot understand why she (and the other young peo-ple) would even want to be members at the "Black" church. There is more than one Slavic evangelical church in the area that she might join if so inclined.

Katia is now a member of the expanding outreach to the Russian-speaking community that this church is sponsoring. At least in her case, those efforts have been successful; now she helps to bring others into the Russian-speaking community within this multiracial congregation. In addition to Russian lan-guage interpretation and headsets during the services, there is also now a service on Friday nights conducted entirely in Russian.

Russian is the unifying language for these recent immigrants from the former Soviet Union, although they come from various regions and a diversity of ethnic backgrounds. Katia explained to me that under the rule of the Communists they were forced to learn Russian in school along with their own ethnic languages. However oppressive this forced assimilation may have been in their countries of origin, the shared language has greatly aided in their coming together and being able to reconstruct a sense of community in the United States, especially in the churches they now find themselves part of as a community of Russian speakers, a state of affairs very similar to that of the Spanish-speaking community within the church.

Katia shared with me that since she was a little girl in Ukraine, she had always known that she would leave the country of her birth and go to live somewhere else in the world. She remembers that in the first grade "something inside" of her made her aware that there was more than the vision of the world the Communists held out to her and her contemporaries. She used to do school projects in which she would pretend to be in another country and "doing something." But she says, "At that time there was no way out . . . the doors were closed . . . you could not even go to another communist country." So when her parents began to consider emigrating from Ukraine to America, she says, "I was the first one . . . begging my parents to come . . . I just wanted to go!"

They made the decision to come to the United States as refugees, fleeing religious persecution. Her parents were Pentecostal. The Pentecostal and Baptist churches operated underground, under cover of night and under the threat of strong, violent repression by the KGB, the Soviet state security service. In order to come together for worship and fellowship, they had to change the locations and times of the home fellowships to keep "one step ahead" of the KGB, who would follow members to try to determine where the meetings were likely to take place. Parents were particularly wary of including their children in these underground fellowships because the repercussions were even harsher if it was learned that parents had brought children to the meetings. Perhaps it was for that reason that Katia did not actually become "born again" until after the family had left the former Soviet Union in 1989 and moved to southern California and later to Sacramento, where she attended a Russian evangelical church freely and openly in the land that has become her new home. She'd always known she would leave Ukraine, and she did.

I wanted to speak with some of the members of the ministry's growing Russian clientele to hear their perspective on several issues. In the Sacramento valley, their presence is being felt increasingly every day. At the local community college, the number of Russian-speaking students is noticeably on the increase. They generally walked and talked together on their way to and from classes. Recently at a local family buffet restaurant my wife and I noticed that the side section was marked "reserved" and a wedding reception was in progress there. The bride and groom were there (in their gown and tuxedo) with all their attendants, guests, children, and elderly, excitedly speaking Russian as they passed to and from the buffets. The rest of us in this inexpensive family restaurant that Saturday afternoon, who were dressed very casually, looked on with interest at our neighbors who had deemed it an acceptable site for an event like a wedding reception. Prosperity, I remember thinking at that moment, might have a different meaning for this group of people from the former Soviet Union, where all-you-can-eat restaurants are probably not among the available choices for dining.

I was particularly interested in learning how Katia experienced the multicultural emphasis at Faith Christian Center as a relatively recent white ethnic immigrant to America. I wanted to hear from this former target of, and now participant in, the church's multiethnic outreach efforts. One of the first questions I asked her concerned how different or similar her religious experience had been before coming to the United States *and* to Faith Christian Center, a ministry with African Americans as the majority cultural group. What was the understanding of American race relations—and of American Blacks—she brought with her to this experience? She responded in terms of what she'd come to appreciate about the United States:

> I think what I came to appreciate [was] the diversity when I came to the United States because it is the most *diversified* nation in the world! I think when I was 15, that's the first time when I saw a Black person, you know? At the age of 15, you know?! It was in Kiev, and Kiev is the capitol of Ukraine and people—like Black people—they came to study over there because we have really good schools over there. So people sometimes move to study over there. But as far as church, like [Mila] said, I think that the spirit is the same—that which unites people. When people from over here go over there, like as the missionary, that's what they experience. They say "We don't know how to speak the language but we appreciate the love of God and the love of the people, you know, the love people have for us and that's what unites us," you know, as one.

I also asked Katia how she felt about being a part of this church, Faith Christian Center. Did she feel comfortable with the things that the church was doing as part of its outreach (with the interpreters, headsets, etc.) to Russian-speaking people and with the much-emphasized multicultural Sunday program? Did she approve of the church's efforts, and when she thought back to when she first came, did she feel more comfortable to hear the Russian language in this church? How did she feel being part of the racial minority as well as being an immigrant? She responded:

> It's different. It's very different. Even though we did not have Black people in Ukraine, there is some kind of prejudism towards [them]. Black people were considered lower-class even though we didn't— we never saw them. I don't know where it came from. I think it comes from the history. People learn history, they know that Black people were put down and that's what they consider them. They see them as lower-class. So, many Russian people that come to the United States, that's what they think, you know? Even right now when—especially older people, you know? They still have that barrier. They still have that wall.
>
> Like when I came to this church my parents could not understand why in the world would I go *to the Black people's church*, you know? It's like . . . *to them, as intelligent people, it was the last thing I could do.* So, still there are misunderstandings, a wall I think. And even right now as we do Russian ministry in the church, it's hard to win people over because—especially older people, younger people are more flexible, they do not have those walls—but older people cannot understand how they can be a part of the church where a lot of people are Black. But we are working on it, and like I said, I myself came to appreciate that. I never was . . . well, I *was* kind of prejudiced too, you know? I thought I wasn't, but I remember the first time I came to Faith Christian Center and they were all in my pew, *they were all Black!* And I felt very strange, you know? I felt like I'm not in this world, you know? I did not feel very comfortable. But God will . . . if you see through God's eyes, you'll come to appreciate his creation, the way it's beautiful.

At one point earlier in the conversation, Katia had mentioned that the experience of Faith Christian Center was also very different for her, in that she had been used to the small, covert, in-house religious meetings in Ukraine (when she'd been allowed to attend at all). This church, with its thousands of members and extensive division of labor was very different from what she'd been used to. Added to this is the fact that the church had an African American pastor, and most of the congregation was African American.

Could she remember what things she witnessed or experienced that were said or done that helped to make her feel that this was a place she could come to accept as "her" church and not just "the Black people's" church?

Yes. Yes, I do, and I think [it was] the people's attitude towards me. The first time I came I almost cried, you know? Because I never had people welcome me that much, you know? Had me stand up, and then give me—whatever—the booklet, and then sing a song to me, and shake my hand—I was overwhelmed! I've never seen anything like that, you know? So, it was kind of like, even though I did not feel comfortable at that time, I think the walls were falling down already, you know? By those things. And also I see that people over here at FCC they do not just talk the gospel, *they live the gospel*. And that's what makes this church different from anything else, from any kind of church.

Asking her to clarify what she meant by "they live the gospel," she replied:

To me, it's when people, when they hear the Word, they *apply* it to their lives. Like when they hear Pastor preach or when they hear the Word of God taught, they use it for their lives. They do not just hear and forget. They use it and they live by it. I saw it. I saw it in many people's lives from Faith Christian Center. And that's really, I think, that's what really destroyed many walls, you know? Because I see those are real people, they're not fake ones, and you don't have even to speak the language to know if the persona is real or fake. You can just know—I don't know how, it's hard to explain—but I think we're made so we can understand. We're made intelligent, you know, we can tell the difference.

Although much of the conversation centered on her experiences in Ukraine and how they compare to her present life, Katia did discuss what she saw as characteristic of the Word of Faith Movement and its message. She had talked about the missionaries to the former Soviet Union and the fact that they seemed to be having much success in attracting the young people into the movement. When asked what she had seen of the Faith teachers and ministers in Ukraine on a recent visit, she had the following to say:

People getting saved. People getting healed . . . that sort of thing. And also Praise and Worship. They have different Praise and Worship. They're not just singing. It's nontraditional singing most of the time, it's more modern most of the time. And it's more upbeat and, I think, it relates more to our times, you know? Where the songs, the more traditional songs, they relate to the past.

And a different style of preaching where it's not anymore just getting up and you sit for 45 minutes, you wait 'til they say "Amen"—

that was my experience with the church. My parents, they are Pentecostal, so I did have a chance to come sometimes—even though they could not take me every time because it was underground—and especially if they found that you brought kids, they would punish you really serious. Prison. You know, so they . . . like most parents if they did not trust [consider it safe] to take their kids [they would not allow them to attend services]. So I was not at the church that much, but sometimes, out of curiosity I would beg my parents to take me. So, I've been there a couple of times, and it was a very traditional church. It was, like, I knew that they were gonna sing three songs. I knew exactly—*exactly*—what's gonna happen, you know? I knew the order, I knew the time, and it never appealed to me—that kind of church—*it never showed the reality.*

Concerning the "different style of preaching," she explained:

These Faith preachers, they do not just take the Word, they take *Rhema*, you know? the Word that *lives*, and they show that word working in their lives. So, they *mix it with their experience* also of the Word, you know? And they do not—like I said—*they take the revelation*, not just the Word—if you take the Word and you don't have any revelation of it, it can be killing—that's what the Bible says, you know? And they, traditional preachers, they cannot . . . I think that's their toughest thing because it's not living in their lives, [so] they cannot relate that, of course, to the hearers. You know, it's like, when you hear that Word and it does not go to your heart, you have a hard time relating to it, and it's like . . . "I hear it, it's good, it's out there . . . *but it's not mine, it's not for me.*" And that's the difference, where when a person has a *revelation* of the Word—when they walk the Word and they relate that with their own experience, *you see that it's real, it's working in their lives, and it can work for you.*

She went on to say that the style in which the minister relates incidents from his or her own life, telling how he or she specifically applies the principles, is useful to her because it shows her that she can use it too. Again, as with most of the other respondents, the practice and application of the message is stressed in her comments.

Katia's discussion of the ideas and images that she and others brought with them to this country as immigrants from the former Soviet Union offers a backdrop to her comments on her reception and understanding of the multicultural program at the church and of the Faith Message. She said that in

Ukraine, while there were few Blacks other than foreign students, there was still prejudice against them, based upon the knowledge that they had been enslaved and second-class citizens in the United States throughout their history here. Her account of coming to this country and going through the process of assimilation, at least partly through the efforts of a predominantly Black church, presents an interesting picture of the way in which religion can act as a mediating factor in the process of interracial integration and acculturation. A common faith—especially in the context of a ministry with a clear goal of "tearing down of the walls" that keep the races separated—provides an ideological medium for the coming-together of the races, at least during the church services and in the context of church-related events and activities.

Katia's articulation of the Faith Message centers on practical application and how the movement's missionaries and churches in the former Soviet Union went about constructing their services, music, and message in such a way as to reach those young people for whom Communism had failed to deliver on its promise to make faith obsolete. She says the message is made "real" by the Faith teachers' "mixing" their revelations of the meanings of the Bible lessons with their own life experience as a way of instructing the congregation in very specific terms, and she contrasts this to the types of religious services she had known in the past. That "old style" of preaching, where the minister might take one scripture and speak on it for an hour, as well as the predictable "pattern" of the order of the service, was also cited as an important difference between the way the Word of Faith Movement teaches and presents the message to its audience and the way the denominational churches do so.

Other Voices, Other Views

Other respondents also had interesting ways of thinking about the Faith Message and how the way things were done at Faith Christian Center differed from what they had been accustomed to in their denominational churches. Some of them focused on the differences in how the messages are *delivered*, the rhetorical, homiletic style of the minister, which they saw as typical and recognizable within the conceptual world built upon the Faith Message. All of those I interviewed said that it was important to them that the Bible was *taught* in the Word of Faith ministry to a much greater extent than in the denominational churches from which they had "come out." Consider the following comments from the interviews with Arlette, a 32-year-old, college-educated, married, African American woman who had come to Faith Christian Center from a local Church of God in Christ (COGIC), a Black Pentecostal denomination of which more than one generation of her family had been members (and some continued to be). She came as a 16-year-old when her mother began visiting and decided to join the ministry, giving Arlette and her younger sister the option of joining as well. She explains some of the ways she would identify whether a television minister was probably of the Word of Faith Movement or not, based upon what she sees and hears:

> The first thing I would notice is that he's not—*he or she*—is not behind the pulpit. In traditional churches the minister is normally behind a pulpit. And the Word of Faith ministers I've seen on TV, they walk back and forth down on the floor with the audience. The second thing I notice is that they—I listen for buzzwords: "prosperity," "faith," "healing," "God's will," et cetera, things like that. Another thing that may clue me in is audience participation, that they involve the audience, the church members, in the sermon. Sometimes they'll have them come up and use them in demonstrations, or they'll go out and talk directly to the audience; whereas, again, in the traditional church that I grew up [in], the pastor was remote and removed—he was elevated above, he was on a platform. Even if it was a smaller church, still the altar, the podium, the pulpit where the pastor dwelled was at least elevated a foot or so.
>
> [In addition to the above]—not to make overgeneralizational statements—a lot of times the [Word of Faith] ministers are younger, and they're dressed more contemporary—they're not as conservative. They may not have robes on—clerical robes. They're more fashionable and in style.

Arlette expresses the fact that for her, reception of the Faith Message does not occur solely with her ears. She is not just listening to the words, but she is also receiving the context in which the message is being delivered. She is listening and also looking at the church, the spatial configuration, the placement of the minister's body relative to the congregation, the average age of the ministers, how they are dressed, as well as a multitude of other visual cues in the setting. For her the inclusion of individuals from the congregation in the minister's demonstrations, helping him to physically enact parts of the message, is also a way to recognize the Faith Message. So reception in this case involves more than just "hearing" the message. It also includes, as part of the overall process, the visually apprehended aspects of the setting and the interactions taking place therein.

Concerning the teachings in the Church of God in Christ, her "first church," Arlette explained that what stood out most for her was the fact that in the traditional church she had been raised in, she had been taught Bible stories, especially Old Testament stories like those of Cain and Abel, David and Goliath, Noah's Ark. Contrasting this with the Faith Message, she said:

> When I came into the Word of Faith, the emphasis was more on *principles* of the Bible, expanding on scripture. It wasn't focusing on tales and fables and stories and things. It was more on principles and structure and how to live your life godly and knowing the will of God for your life and knowing who you are in Christ, et cetera.

Concerning which parts of the Faith Message attracted her or convinced her to switch her affiliation, she had this to say:

> I honestly can't say that it was the Faith Message *all alone* because when [at age 16] I rededicated my life to Christ—meaning that I received salvation and gave—you know—came back to wanting to serve God fully and not just do my own thing, I had already started crying out to God wanting more of him, wanting more fullness to understand him better. And I remember distinctly saying to God that there has to be more to him than what I was learning. There had to be more than just Bible stories; there had to be more than just the things that I had heard in Sunday school. And I already had a preestablished hunger, a preexisting hunger to know more about God than what I felt I was getting. I felt that even after 16 years of growing up in that particular denomination, things were still *limited*. I still felt that God was being limited, that there had to be more; that he wasn't confined to what I heard all of my life. So when I went to the Word of Faith Movement, and I heard about how they were teaching scriptures and teaching in the Word, teaching you how to pray even, and teaching you effective prayer life, those were things that already—resonated with an already existing hunger. Coming into the Word of Faith, I was being taught things at that particular time that I was hungering for. *They were addressing my hunger.*

In a way similar to what Cassandra and many other interviewees related, Arlette wanted more than what she was getting in the religious doctrine and subsequent life experiences she had been familiar with prior to being introduced to the Faith Message. Arlette expressed that she had already been dissatisfied with what she was learning or hearing in her former church. It was no longer meeting her perceived needs, and once she found a church that did so, those old loyalties to the congregation of her youth weakened as she moved on. Again, the word *limit* is being used to explain that for many people, the decision to switch their affiliation to a Faith Movement church, and the Faith Message, was based upon its teaching, which they felt helped them to escape limitations that may have been part of their ascribed social location.

The theme of personal empowerment is again echoed in these comments. Arlette also comments on the spatial configuration of the churches she has come to know as Faith Movement churches, as seen on television. She mentions that in the traditional churches she had grown up in, the pastor was elevated above the congregation and the pulpit behind which he stood was on a platform. This image stands in contrast to the Faith teachers, who are frequently seen walking down on the floor among the congregation, invoking the image of Jesus walking among the common folk and teaching them. She also noted that, to her, the Faith teachers tend to be younger and better dressed (more "in style") than ministers in the traditional churches she had known.

Another respondent, Jon, a mobile home and real estate salesman in his mid-thirties, offered a particularly interesting description of how he recognized a Faith teacher, or someone preaching the Faith Message, when he encountered one on television. He too used visual cues to help him recognize the message and the movement within the spatial configuration of the setting in which the doctrine was taught, but he also drew upon other aspects of the setting. He explains:

> If I was to see a preacher come on, how would I recognize it? I think the color and the architecture of the church is the first thing that might set me off. And then, possibly . . . possibly a more upbeat message. That's about it.

When asked to elaborate on the "color and architecture" point he continued:

> Well, let's see: I see the architecture as being . . . the colors of the carpet being bright—I see a lot of blues, reds in the carpet . . . some gold trim, woodwork, a lot of round, theater-type . . . newer—I see newer buildings. And I see that with a couple [of] other churches, but not as many—I see the Word of Faith has quite a few.

When this same man was asked to compare the Faith Message to his earlier religious background, his responses again included visual imagery:

> Okay, Catholicism was the religion I was born, or baptized, under. I say it this way: my religious life and my spiritual life with Catholicism was dead, and my spiritual life with the Word of Faith is alive. I began to reflect on my life as a Catholic, and at times I have visions of heavy darkness and actually tremble at what spirits I was in

the middle of. I see the Catholic teaching and such as a manmade set of traditions, and I see the Word of Faith as a Bible-oriented faith, an educated faith, an enlightened faith, where each person has a communication directly to the throne. [In] Catholicism you talk to a man who intercedes for you. And I see Catholicism being full of idol worship, if you want to call it [that]. Idolatry, I guess you would. And I don't see that in the Word of Faith. I don't see that. I see the Word of God being the highest icon or highest piece of material or highest reference. I saw [Catholicism] also as a very gloomy doctrine. Gloomy, dark colors—black, dark colors.

Two other respondents also remarked that they saw a pattern or characteristic design in how Word of Faith Movement churches are constructed or at least decorated. One of them mentioned that when she had first come to visit the "old" church (next door to the present, newer structure) many years ago, one of the things that stood out for her was the colors—rich burgundy, gold, that she took to be the "church colors"—especially since she'd also seen a female church member with pompoms in matching colors. These two spoke of how the Bible ascribes meaning to certain colors as representing royalty, for example. They all received the message as part of an inclusive gestalt of concept, light, color, sound, form, and other elements. This suggests a more complex model of what goes into the process of making meaning of religious belief; it is not merely a matter of cognitive or spiritual sense making; there are other, extratextual elements that must be considered and understood as well.

The fact that members identify the colors and architecture of the church as clues as to whether they are seeing a Word of Faith movement minister on television raises an interesting question. Those ministries wealthy enough to have national and international broadcasts are the ones that people come to know and more readily recognize. Thus those ministries seen on television probably put more effort into the decoration of their sanctuaries because they have become virtual sets or sound stages upon which the television broadcast or performance takes place. Before the church began taping services for broadcast several years ago, the sanctuary at Faith Christian Center was nicely decorated, but with the introduction of cameras and extra-bright lights that were turned on at a certain time in the service, the sanctuary was transformed and changed into something else, a set for a televised production. The people in the service were not only believers sitting in a Sunday morning service, they also became people "on television" simultaneously.[1]

The churches seen on television are perhaps setting the trends that smaller churches seek to emulate in designing their sanctuaries. For example, the motif of international flags decorating the walls in several Word of Faith Movement churches, as well as in the sanctuaries on television broadcasts, can be seen in photographs of Kenneth Hagin's and Kenneth Copeland's churches. The broadcasting of church services may be communicating more than just the messages being preached. This was obviously the case with these respondents, whose first thoughts in relating their understanding of the Faith Message were rendered in visual terms and included such things as color, decoration, the style of ministers' dress, and their placement relative to the people they are speaking to.

Still another respondent singled out the structure of the message in describing how he might recognize a television minister if presented with one. Martin, an instructional aide in his early thirties, had the following to say:

> Okay, I would look for multiple references right back to the Word. Right back-to-back. I mean maybe within a ten- to fifteen-minute period. Maybe six direct references—like "turn to this [scriptural passage]" and maybe a few seconds or minutes of elaboration and then "let's look at [another scripture]." As opposed to another religion or maybe another type of Christianity where they could have one overlying reference and then just have a whole service about that one reference and just elaborate over and over. That's one thing I look for.

When I probed further, asking if there were anything else he would use to recognize the Faith Message, his response was one of the most interesting and insightful of all that I heard. He pointed out the way in which the Faith Message is shaped by its teachers' understanding that what they are teaching has many critics—even from within the charismatic movement of which they are also part. Martin's comments here show that even ordinary audience members—those who may never have taken a seminary homiletics course—can still see and *hear* that this external discourse has been structured into the very messages themselves.

Martin also noticed some common patterns in the *attitude* toward those who would disagree with the teachings of those within the movement. Describing what he thinks of as defensiveness on the part of the Faith teachers, he refers to a "cockiness" in the attitude of many of the most prominent Word of Faith personalities that comes through in their presentation of the message. He describes it this way:

> Yeah, a certain kind of attitude makes them act in a way that they feel they're on one side or they have to be on the defensive. As op-

posed to other denominations or religions where they are really over with it and they don't have a right line of defense because they don't really feel they have direct opposition in what they're saying. That's one thing I look for: the people who preach their teachings in a way that they're willing to "punch out" anybody—oh, so to speak, "punch out"—punch out anybody who is in opposition to this [teaching].

It's aggressive! They [denominational ministers] have a sense, to me, of being passive, where they don't come in there already knowing somebody's gonna disagree with them. They come in there feeling that it's objective truth and that's gonna defend itself, and they don't have to defend it because it's gonna be absolute. And it's gonna cut through anything—it's gonna cut like a knife. So they can be, in a sense "passive," but the Faith teachers . . . they're aggressive with that thing because . . . they're on the defensive—they feel like there's always gonna be somebody in opposition to this doctrine or that doctrine or this teaching, and they come prepared—already in advance knowing they're gonna just be teaching this on one hand, but defending it later on down the line. And maybe they're thinking maybe somewhere down the line they'll come up with a new revelation—really profound and new, and with it being new, there's gonna be a lot of people not really buying it, and knowing that, they're gonna have a real aggressive defense to the teaching planned. It's a whole complex thing. It's more complex than just a simple message and simple truth and you just receive it because it's absolutely true and it makes you feel good because the truth sets you free. It's more complex than that—it's defensive, aggressive. It's like they think of strategic defense plans in advance and they already have, *as part of their message,* some of the reasoning to defend this.

So, for Martin, it is very apparent that the rebuttals to detractors' criticisms are actually structured into the teaching. He goes on to explain it this way:

A lot of the messages have a—it['s] already complex and built in, you know, the rebuttal and the—preconceived defenses—for this profound teaching they're gonna have. This profound teaching that's gonna, in their words, "knock over a sacred cow." And here's another thing: you know, it's because . . . now, now, maybe I never assigned—the label "traditional values" with the *other* denominations, but maybe because—maybe the fact that other denominations tend to line [up] in the traditional ways, traditional Judeo-Christian, and maybe because they line up with that, there's no new revelation, there's new ways of thinking about old revelations, but there are no new revelations. Maybe they feel because of that they don't have to *defend* anything because it's already there—it's not anything new, it's not reinventing the wheel. It's just there and it's just a new way of thinking about it that will, maybe, break it down for somebody else, you know, thinking about in a whole new way. But in this—denomination of the Word of Faith, there's always a new revelation, a new—profound—never-yet-heard-before revelation. And sometimes those new revelations are hard to grasp. And because they deviate from traditional views—Judeo[-Christian] views, they have to be prepared with already-made defenses. Strategic plans, you know—they gotta come in there with the defense as part of the package—or at least have a defense ready later on when somebody else hears this new revelation, and it's not widely accepted. Have your defense ready—so I kinda get that from the messages, and I look for that. I can use that to determine if this is some Faith teaching. It's really a *sensitive* thing, but I can pick it up. And it's what I can use to determine "Oh, this is basically Word of Faith," and use that to kinda determine if this is *not* Word of Faith teaching.

Martin's observations brought into sharp focus an extremely important element of the Faith Message: the attitude that accompanies its presentation and reinforces it as a distinct worldview. The Faith Message is Christianity "with attitude," to borrow a popular expression. This attitude is based on the belief in believers' "knowing who they are" in Christ and the sense of entitlement that flows from it. There are even some Faith teachers within the movement who proclaim that born again Christians are "little-g" gods and until they accept the reality of who they are in Christ, they will never be able to access the power and the privileges inherent in their God-given status. This attitude is also an outgrowth of the Faith Movement's belief that it has a revelation of the truth that makes its churches more advanced than the denominational churches.[2] This theme runs throughout the world of the Word of Faith Movement; the way those ideas come to shape not only the structure of the message but its delivery as well is just as Martin has described. The Faith Message is aggressive, it is practical and instrumental, it is personally empowering, its delivery is "cocky"—it is all of these. These comments demonstrate the richness and variety to be found in individuals' accounts of what resonates for them about even so different a cultural product as religious doctrine.

We have heard from several individuals who are part of the rank and file of the Word of Faith Movement as well as of their local church. They each come with their own background, experience, and vision of what the Faith Message means to them, and they express those meanings in various ways. Before leaving this chapter it is necessary to summarize some of what we have heard here and begin to think about the larger implications of each part.

This chapter has primarily been about how people bring their own personal lenses to bear on their descriptions and account of their understanding of the Faith Message. Without exception, every one of those interviewed explained their understanding of the Faith Message in terms of what it was not—that is, in terms of how it was different from the denominational teachings they had known or grown up with prior to hearing the particular brand of Christianity that led to their decision to switch to a church that taught the Faith Message. Cassandra, Russell, Katia, and the others said they were able to recognize the Faith Message when they heard it by virtue of the fact that it was a positive message that focused the minds of the listeners on what they could do or be *today*, in this world, rather than merely waiting to get to heaven. They spoke of the Faith Message as being a teaching of victory, how to win in their lives, and they said that the Word of Faith Movement churches seemed to be more organized and structured than the denominational churches they had all been a part of. One of the of most frequently invoked of all the themes used in describing the Faith Message was that it was practical, a message that begged to be used and applied to the improvement of one's own life and circumstances as well as those of one's loved ones.

The use of one's faith to provide a sense of personal empowerment was another persistent theme. Some conceived of and described the Faith Message in terms of the spatial layout and decoration of the Word of Faith Movement churches where they saw and heard it taught. Others singled out the style with which the minister delivered the message: aggressively, defensively, with the rebuttal to expected criticisms already built into the message. In all, there were a number of ways people said they could recognize the Faith Message when they heard it.

But if we were to pinpoint a single motivation to explain why they came to the Word of Faith Movement and adopted its teachings, it would have to be (as they each expressed directly or indirectly) that *they wanted more.* Repeatedly, respondents said they wanted more from their Christian experience, their Christian walk, than they were getting (or taught to even desire or expect) in their former churches or what they knew about Christianity prior to hearing this message.

The central motif in this chapter has been the diversity and variety of aspects and elements people find salient to their own understanding and recognition of the Faith Message when they encounter it. It is not only the content of the Message, it is also the way the ministers do not stand behind the pulpit; the way the churches are decorated in bright colors as a function of the fact that many of them are the sets for television broadcasts; the way color and light also function as aesthetic demonstration of revelation, bringing light or enlightenment, versus the drab, dark traditions one respondent noted when he thought of his background in the Catholic Church; the way the delivery of the message is aggressive and carries within it a built-in rebuttal to the criticism its teachers know is being directed at them from the conservative doctrinal "center," which has defined it as heretical; and the way the teaching expresses an ethos of personal empowerment, encouraging and sanctifying individual mobility beyond certain limitations on one's thinking and behavior that are based upon their past or present socioeconomic status. But one of the most compelling themes to emerge out of this look at what members see as most relevant in their descriptions of the contours of the Faith Message concerns the degree to which they use their backgrounds—what they brought with them from their past religious or life experience—to help them to make sense of the doctrine for themselves in new contexts.

Among these respondents, the meaning of the Faith Message was derived not only from the specific, expressed content of the message but also from what is not specifically part of the content of the doctrine. Together their experiences suggest that the process of deriving meaning from an object is much more complicated and involves attention to many more criteria than commonly thought. This process is not necessarily confined to what is verbalized and apparently does, but can, involve a reckoning of extratextual nonverbal clues as well.

Finally, the Faith Message has meaning that is *relative* to other forms of doctrine that individuals were acquainted with prior to contact with it. Most of these respondents came from other churches where things were quite different from what they found in a Word of Faith Movement church. The variety of ways with which they first approached and understood (and continue to approach and understand) the Faith Message have been shaped in, through, and against their understanding of the characteristics they associate with the denominational churches they have left behind.[3]

2

Living the Faith Message

Work out your own salvation in fear and trembling.

—Philippians 2:12

At one point in our interview, Arlette caught me off guard with one of her responses. As unexpected as her response was at the time, though, it seemed to crystallize in just a few words her understanding of and application of the Faith Message. I had told her that I would read half of a statement and asked her to respond by completing the sentence. The exercise went like this:

INTERVIEWER   "Now that I know who I am in Christ . . ."

RESPONDENT   "I don't have to take any *crap*."

Arlette went on to explain that she was thinking of her interactions with other people, with the Devil, and in the context of negative situations and in general, the storms of life, including the "curse" of sickness, disease, or poverty. This young African American woman was stating her claim and expressing her understanding of her identity as a Christian. To use Kenyon's expression, she did not see herself as being just a "merely saved" Christian but as a powerful, overcoming one, with rights and privileges accruing. Knowing who she is in Christ means not having to "take any crap." How does this notion of knowing who you are as a Christian, in addition to other specific teachings that make up the Faith Message, translate into everyday behavior? What does the relation between abstract belief and observable practice tell us about the way religion is embodied in believers' lives? And how do people of faith reconcile their ideas about how to live out their own understandings of their faith against what they are being taught by other, interested, parties like ministers and others who assume responsibility for their souls?

There is a more or less official reading of the Faith Message that is espoused and encouraged in their local churches. What people say they actually *do* with it however, how it shapes their everyday lives, does not necessarily follow. When we look at how believers come to their own practical understandings and attempts to live out their faith, the twin themes of struggle and ambivalence emerge. At the level of practice, they actively struggle over, against, with, around, and through the doctrinal readings coming from respected authority figures in the movement at large and in their church (as well as from other members). They also struggle against the readings of movement outsiders and critics as they try to make sense of who they are as Christians, what they believe, and how to live it in practical ways in a very contingent world.

Cassandra: "I think about who I am in Christ, and I have a right to be there like anybody else!"

Cassandra explained how she thinks her life has changed in the more than 13 years since she became a member of the Word of Faith Movement and was first exposed to the notion of "knowing who you are in Christ":

> I would say my life is *better*. I'm more apt to branch out into areas that are unfamiliar to me. And that stems from my confidence in knowing who I am in Christ. For instance, I play golf. I started in '96. But there are times—even to this day—when I go out on the golf course, and I still feel a little bit uneasy because I may be the only African American out there and the only African American *woman* because it's primarily a male sport—*white male* sport. But I don't let that stop me. Because again I think about who I am in Christ, and I have a right to be there like anybody else [slapping the table for emphasis]. And I go. I go out there no matter—even if I feel uneasy when I first get there, I still go.
>
> Maybe there was a time in my life when I wouldn't have. Especially living in Oakland, in primarily the inner city. [It was] primarily Black. I went to all-Black schools—*everything was Black*. Coming to

Sacramento was very different for me. So I think if I didn't know who I was in Christ, and I had all that limited thinking and I thought a lot about what other people thought about me as an African American woman, I think that would keep me from doing the things I enjoy doing. And so my knowing who I am in Christ has blown that out. But it doesn't mean I don't get those uneasy feelings when I go into a setting, that I'm "the only one." You know, I still get some of that, but I don't let that stop me.

Providing a specific example of how she draws upon this knowledge of who she is in Christ in the type of situation she has just alluded to, she explains:

I remember . . . when I do it, I'm thinking "Okay, God, what're we gon' do? Okay, Father, I'm going in here." "Now . . ." (I start talking to him, and I say) ". . . you know I deserve to be here just like the next person. You created all of this and I'm your child. No one has a monopoly on this." And I'm telling myself—I'm saying this as I'm walking through those doors—still looking at all of these faces looking at *me*. And I'm smiling, because I know who I am. I say "Okay, Father, I know you're here" and that's what I do for me. And people respond to me. They don't respond to this little queasiness in my stomach—they don't know anything about that, only I'm feeling that. They just see the smile on my face—this woman looks like "Oh, Okay," and then people begin to respond. I'm like "Okay, Lord." And so that's what I do. *It's the power of who I am in Christ.* That's what it is. I don't know any other way to explain it.

Throughout our conversation, Cassandra's responses expressed her sense of empowerment and ability, with the aid of her understanding of the teachings of the Word of Faith Movement, to push past limitations—whether in terms of her own thinking or of specific life experiences. The expansion past limited thinking is a defining characteristic for the way she understands and applies this part of the teaching in her own life. She felt as though she was no longer put "in a box" in certain contexts as a consequence of being African American, a woman, and from a certain socioeconomic background.

Although her own background may be "foreign" to the traditional image of the world of golf (white males of the middle and upper classes), and her prior experiences may have been shaped in an all-Black environment, she is able to draw upon the teaching concerning knowing who you are in Christ to provide for herself a liturgical justification and even a sense of *entitlement* to be in this environment. She uses this concept to be able to enter and survive in an environment in which others without a similar reservoir of self-affirmation might feel uncomfortable (as she admitted herself) and might allow that discomfort to keep them from moving forward into new realms of experience to which her education and professional status have given her access. She says she "deserves to be there, just like anybody else" because of her belief that God made "all this" and that, as his child, she has full authority to go wherever she wishes among whomever she encounters. Hers is an excellent example of this teaching applied, put to work, in an individual's day-to-day experience. It also serves as an example of the way the teaching of the Word of Faith Movement encourages self-actualization and upward socioeconomic mobility while supplying a belief system that supports that process. This belief system and the accompanying worldview provide followers with a message of personal empowerment that helps them negotiate the potential tension or sense of dislocation and alienation that may arise as their social class mobility begins to bring them to social and cultural environments that may be vastly different from those of their own origins.

Russell: "They say, 'Are you going to get a flu shot?' No. Why I gotta inoculate myself against something that I'm not gonna get?"

In the few hours we talked, Russell provided several quite remarkable illustrations of the actual practice of positive confession among members of the Word of Faith Movement. We've already seen how he trained his dog, Lucy, by "speaking over" her only positive words that affirmed the behavioral characteristics that he wanted to see manifested in her. His description of how positive confession shaped his everyday experience and interactions with nonbelievers was also instructive. He explains his understanding of the concept:

> The Bible says that when I speak, my words have power. The Bible says in the book of Proverbs that "death and life are in the power of the tongue." By speaking positive I'm speaking life. By speaking negative I'm speaking death. An easy example of that is, I hear on a regular basis in this time of year, from about October to February, it's what they say quote flu and cold season. And they say, are you going to get a flu shot? No. Why I gotta inoculate myself against something that I'm not gonna get? Doesn't mean symptoms won't come. So the power of positive confession says that "by his stripes I was healed." If I *was*, then I *am* and I *will be*. So it's not flu and cold

season, it's health season. Okay? I just reach out and grab more health 'cause I'm already well.

There might be a recession. Well, a recession is something secular. The Bible says I can prosper. Whatever I put my hand to prospers, so my positive confession is that all my needs are met. I've even stopped praying that. I don't pray about my needs anymore because the Bible says if I seek first the kingdom of God and his righteousness he'll meet my needs. Therefore, I now pray and thank God for my wants and my desires being met, because my needs are already done. So, I'm not denying the fact that I have a need, but my basic everyday—my bills are paid. Money's in the bank. Money cometh to me, right now!

Russell's comments articulate the very heart of the position of the Faith Message on claiming prosperity and believing that it is indeed God's will to supply every need (and as some would say, desire) of his children, born-again Christians. Russell admits to the objective fact that he has a need rather than denying the reality of a negative circumstance as, for example, Christian Science might lead some believers to do with respect to physical illness. Rather, by thanking God *in advance* for the need already being met, Russell sees himself as exercising his faith in an act of affirming a promised outcome: that all the things believers need to survive and to prosper will be supplied by God. The promises of God as found in scripture are taken to be the source of Russell's claim to having all his financial needs met.

Throughout the foregoing excerpts there are examples in which he is actually using positive confession as he is speaking to me. His last declaration—"money cometh to me, right now"—was one of the corporate and individual confessions that had been given to the congregation during the week-long Finance Convention discussed earlier (that is, they were instructed to shout it together at various points throughout the week and use it as their own personal declaration). Russell's use of it in the context of our discussion was a way of invoking a meaning we both presumably shared. It also illustrates the fact that in Word of Faith Movement churches certain confessions become conventional and part of the everyday vocabulary that congregation members use in conversation with each other. Several of the phrases he used can be found, more or less verbatim, in any number of books and sermons and the everyday speech of the pastor and other members within the subculture of the Word of Faith Movement.

He says he does not pray to God anymore about his needs because, by faith, he believes that all of his needs are met, which then leaves him free to pray to God for the "over and above," the things he wants in this life. This is yet another illustration of the way many movement members are taught to apply the Faith Message's teachings. Let us not misunderstand what Russell is saying here: his confession is that his needs are already met, so he can then pray and thank God in advance that his desires are being met also. He said earlier that God's promises are conditional, so it is not that he expects to receive whatever he wants from God without first living up to his understanding of God's will. Some critics charge that people in the Word of Faith Movement are using God as a sort of genie or servant whose sole function is to do their bidding.

I asked Russell to provide a specific example of his application of positive confession in the midst of a specific situation in his personal life, past or present:

> Real easy. Okay. When we changed employers and moved back into the job market and I was putting together resumes trying to find out where I was supposed to be employed. And I went out on job interviews and prayed and asked God. I thought that a particular employer was where I was supposed to go to work. But that didn't work out and I sent a resume to the employer that I work for now, and they responded and told me by answer machine that to work for them I had to go through an agency. I was already working for that agency. So the agency called and said, if you want this position this is what it is. You can go to work. So I went to work on a Wednesday, and my confession on the day that I went to work was "This is going to be my job. God is my source and not this employer, and God will meet my needs." And there's a number of individuals that were brought on board as a temporary at the same time as I was. Well, I'm now on staff. I've been hired by this company. I've been picked up by the company 'cause I kept saying, God, I believe that this is my job. God, I believe you sent me here. God, I believe that if I do what is right before you, then you will take care of me. And you have, and I did everything that I knew to do by meeting the criteria, the standards of the company. And the Bible says that I have to do what I can do in order for God to do what he'll do. And I kept telling people, "You know I'm gonna get hired. I'm gonna get hired. Watch and see. I'm gonna get hired."

Notice how Russell was applying positive confession in the everyday context of his job search. He recounted that he began to pray and talk to God about the position that he was doing as an temporary employee, "confessing" that it already was his permanent job. He also explained that he actually took great pains to meet the company's hiring criteria and work standards as a temporary employee, but the most compelling example of the practice of positive confession in this story was that he kept telling *other* people that he was going to be hired by the company. That is the distinction between publicly "confessing" something and privately praying for it to come to pass ("*if* it be God's will"). The act of voicing to others those things one is "believing (God) for" (to give them or do on their behalf) is taught in the Faith Message to be an act of faith, opening one's self up to potential ridicule by unbelievers and daring to take that risk because of their faith that God will not let one down.

Positive confession is not simply prayer. It is certainly not the type of quiet, contemplative prayer in which one communes with the sacred in silence or in private. The practice of positive confession, as expressed in this example, is enlivened through the faithful going about and telling other people what they are believing God for. Russell was, in effect, "naming" what he wanted (a particular job) and "claiming" that job as his, even as he continued in his position as a temporary worker employed by an agency. According to the Faith Message, the boldness of his words were, by faith, helping to create the situation in the supernatural or spiritual realm that he desired to see manifest in the natural realm of existence and experience. Continuing with his anecdote:

INTERVIEWER   And what'd they say?

RUSSELL   "Well . . . uh . . . yeah, yeah!" [mockingly]. A lot of negative confession. One of the things that the warehouse manager told me was, the reason he was hiring me or putting me on their payroll was twofold: number one, my work record, the fact that I don't miss—I haven't missed a day since I started there. I not only did the work in the area that I was assigned, but I also volunteered to work in other areas of the company in order to get some extra hours in. The company is a very well-known distribution company in the food industry. But, within the food service industry there's a lot of pressure. There isn't a lot of profit individually. The markup is very low, so you make money on volume. You don't make it individually. It's very pressure oriented. Because of that there's a whole lot of people that don't understand that, you know, the prices of it. Therefore, they look at it from an employee standpoint. "They're overworking me. They're working me too hard."

So they're always saying negative things about the company. And I kept saying, "No, no, no. It doesn't have to be that way. You know, God will give you favor." In fact, somebody told me yesterday that, you know, how come I got the line that I'm selecting on, on products? You know it's a very easy line. And I said, you know, "The reason I'm on this line is because I have favor." You know, I have favor with God, and God takes care of me. And because I have favor with God, that's why I was picked up, and the manager told me that [it was] because I didn't think negative when other people did, because I always had a positive attitude.

Russell's account provides us with another look into the culture of the Word of Faith Movement and the worldview it teaches and encourages its followers to apply in the most mundane situations, infusing the profane with sacred significance in their lives. The foregoing example illustrates how he put into practice the teaching of positively confessing the desired result and the fact that he attributed the end to that very practice. His belief was bolstered by the fact that his manager had told him his positive attitude was what secured his job for him: that when everyone else was thinking and speaking negatively, he remained positive *and* a hard worker in the face of uncertainty.

Russell talked about having favor with God and having actually "confessed" that favor, based upon another often-quoted scriptural promise that believers would have favor with God and man. At the time of these interviews, the pastor had recently published a book on the subject of favor, so it was a regularly cited topic in the church and in many of the messages at the time. Accordingly, I found that this concept crept into the comments of many of the interviewees. So it is not just the speaking of the desired result but also taking corresponding action that is shown in this example. People in the movement are often criticized for going around "speaking to things" and expecting them to be manifest according to their will. But several respondents in this study spoke of positive confession in a way that demonstrated their understanding that speaking was not enough to make things manifest; their subsequent actions had to be aligned with what they were "speaking for" and "believing for"—and they understood that they still might not get what they desired. They did not see it as some sort of "magic formula" or incantation, as critics of the movement and this particular part of its teachings often charge.

Before leaving this discussion of the experience of positive confession, let us hear from Arlette again. She told me that she had saved up a little anecdote to share with me concerning an experience she had once had in a Word church. For a particular holiday service she had been asked to work with a group of women for the presentation of a special song. She was working with a large group in the church, teaching them the song that they were to perform during the upcoming service. She had been a member of the church for many years and had even been a member of the choir and other groups that sang in the ministry. Her story illustrates the way positive confession shapes the boundaries of acceptable speech—even in a song performed in the course of the service, where everything that takes place is thought to be part of "ministering" to the spirits of all in attendance. Describing this incident, she says:

> The night of the first rehearsal I received the words. I did not know the song. So I received the words, and I was looking at the words. It was [the contemporary gospel singer] John P. Kee's "Strength," and there was one particular line that said [God gives me] "strength to suffer," and the warning signs went off in my mind. I said "Oh, no, these women here are not gonna buy that." So I went to the orga- nizers, the ones who had asked me [to participate]. I went to one of them, the young ladies, and I showed her the line, and I said "Do you want to keep this?" and she said "yeah, they *need* to know how to suffer." So I was fine. But then when we taught the song, I could see—I was watching the ladies, and I could see their faces—and they were just not having it, they were not in agreement. So, then, finally, the other woman that had asked me to participate came up and whispered in my ear. She said, "Let's change it." I said "How 'bout 'strength to prosper?'"—'cause I knew the attitude. I knew these people, without knowing them individually; I knew the tenor of the church. She said, "Yeah, that's fine." So when I told them to "scratch out *suffer* and put *prosper*," the wild jubilation just went up! You know, "Yeah, yeah" kind of exclamations, "Yeah!" So *then* they were able to sing the song. Before, singing something like "strength to suffer" was just not—*they were not having that.*

After hearing this story, I wondered what Arlette thought had happened to the themes of suffering and endurance through difficult times (not to men- tion the notion of eschewing material gain in favor of spiritual blessing) that are seen in the stories of many of the most revered Old and New Testament figures and traditionally thought to be important mechanisms God uses to build his people's character. The theme of suffering and self-denial—especially suffering unjustly and in place of those who are guilty, as Christ did—is central to traditional forms of Christianity but seems to have been redefined by the Word of Faith movement. To my question "What happened to *suffering* and *endurance* through hard times?" she quickly replied:

> They've been banished to denominational thought. You know, suf- fering is not part of the Word of Faith teaching. It's like, if you suf- fer, it's only gonna be a light affliction, which is but for a moment, because it's working for eternal, exceeding glory. It's only a *stepping-*

stone to get you to a greater glory. Even if you do suffer, you're gonna come out on top and all right, and better than you were before. So, it's like a gnat, it's just a little *inconvenience* to your greater good.

I probed further, asking her to explain, from her understanding of the dominant view within the movement, what it meant if someone was experiencing *ongoing* suffering and hardship over an extended period of time. How might it be interpreted in terms of one's belief in positive confession and thinking and the resulting circumstances in the believer's life? Again, she replied with little hesitation:

Well, they must be out of the will of God . . . you know, that's the kind of thing. You must be out of the will of God; you must have given place to the Devil. So, you know, suffering as conventionally taught by churches—especially mainstream Black churches—has no place in the Word of Faith teaching. It's just totally out line with the Word that's being taught there. So suffering has to take a back-step— basically, it has to get "under your feet," as we're being taught. It has to be placed under your feet. So there's a lot of, like, overturning of things that are in the conventional or traditional churches—a lot of things have been overturned. Things that even today, like, the first church holds fast to. Like you said suffering, like, you know there's gonna be a greater good at the end, but in the Faith churches, you do not stay at suffering for long—you *shouldn't* stay in suffering long. Where in the traditional church, if you have somebody suffering, you have your saints over there praying for them, bringing them food—whatever it may be—if somebody's sick the [Church] Mother's over there praying and things like that and people are there to see you *through* it, and that—in the Faith church it's like your suffering better be for [only] a moment—you go and get you some Intercessory prayer [clapping hands together], *prayer warriors,* and it's all over.

I asked, "So, who is to blame if suffering does *not* end shortly?" Arlette answered:

You! Basically. Your faith must not have been strong enough, you must have been outside the will of God, you must have let The Enemy [Satan] in somewhere, you must not know the Word. Something. It's *your* fault. [Because if you knew the Word] you would be able to banish that demon and change your circumstance, and end

your suffering. You can *confess* your way into healing; *confess* your
way into all type of victory, [so] it must be your fault. You must not
be praying the appropriate prayer that availeth much.

When I asked her if there was any more to the story, she replied:

No, that was basically it. Just to see that one word could change the
whole attitude of a [singing group]. You know, one word could bring
gloomy looks, and one word could change all that gloom into jubila-
tion.

I wanted her to elaborate on what she thought was the source of the "gloom,"
the hesitation of the people to sing a song that contained the lyric "[God gives
me] strength to *suffer*." She explained:

That's negative confession. Suffering and things like that—"strength
to suffer"—that could basically be a negative [confession]. God
doesn't want to give you strength to suffer. You know, there's an old
song, "God, don't move my mountain but give me the strength to
climb," but now the Faith church would tell you if you have faith the
size of a mustard seed, you can tell that *mountain* to be removed. So
you don't have to climb, you don't have go through the wilderness,
you don't have to go through valleys, you can *speak* to your valleys
and tell 'em to become, you know, plains and pastures.

Here we have another example of a respondent structuring her discussion
of the Word of Faith movement and its teachings and practices directly in
relation to the denominational "first church" in which she had grown up. I
wanted her to assess for me the impact her experience with the two world-
views—the "Give me strength to climb" orientation of the denominational
church versus the "Remove the mountain" attitude of the Word of Faith movement—has had thus far on her life and practice.

I believe I've kinda come full circle to where I'm kinda like "Okay, I
may have been in the church that taught me "Give me strength to
climb," now I've come to a church that tells me to tell the mountain
to "Move, get thou hence," you know, "Get outta here." But now I
feel like I'm in the middle, somewhere in the middle. I can't really
define it, but I'm somewhere in between the two where I can appreciate what I'm being taught in the Faith churches. I can adhere to
that. But I can also appreciate what I was taught in my "first"
church and adhere to *that,* and come somewhere in the middle and
gain a happy medium so that *if* a trial comes, if suffering comes,

I'm not thrown off course or being made to think that God doesn't love me or I must be in sin. So it's *balance*. I guess it's what I mean to say. Balance seems to be coming into my life where I don't feel like I'm a dirty dog or anything if there is a trial. And I can still hold fast to the word of God and be able to incorporate some of the things I've been taught about prayer and intercession and positive confession (if we have to call it that). So being able to find a happy medium between the two.

I asked whether she had found it problematic to be taught to "Speak and remove" the mountain, as opposed to the "Give me strength to climb" orientation to problems and suffering, and whether she has been able to just tell the mountains in her life to "move." To this she replied:

No. I have mountains in my life right now. And it *does* become problematic in that [I] feel like maybe I'm not praying right, maybe I'm not praying the appropriate prayer. Maybe if you see something in your life that you know needs correcting, and it's not being corrected, sometimes you will question yourself and question your faith and find yourself running back to God—" God, what part of the recipe did I miss? What part of the recipe am I overlooking? [Interviewer: "The formula"] Yeah, exactly. What part did I not apply—did I not say "in Jesus' name?" It's like "What did I miss the first time?" So you find yourself in conflict sometimes because you feel like "Okay, I'm doing everything they told me to do, then why isn't this working?"

So you're finding out that God isn't just a workhorse God. You know, there's still some things . . . He's a sovereign God, and there're some things sometimes that—you don't put a quarter in and get a can of soda out. Sometimes there's a waiting period. There're just different degrees of life. You may be in a place in your life where maybe you can't handle what you really think you want and what you really need. So, yes, it can be problematic because you can find yourself questioning your faith, questioning your position in God, questioning the prayers that you prayed—were they really fervent, were they really effective, were they really in line with God? Or just being quiet sometimes and realizing that God is not always . . . he's not just a formulaic God—that if I just pray this prayer, then this will immediately occur for me. Just learning God, really. Learning what he's about and his timing. You know, I was taught in the first church there's timing. God's timing is not our timing. And although we may want something when we want it, and although we may pray this prayer, the *perfect* prayer, doesn't mean that we'll necessarily receive it at that moment. So it can be very conflictual.

Arlette is ambivalent. She has found that in her attempts to reconcile the two contrasting visions of what the Christian life should be like, tensions and conflict arise. She says this leads her not to rely too heavily on what either side—her "first church" or the Word of Faith Movement—has taught her but that she must go to God for herself for the answers that make sense to her in the context of a particular life situation. In the years since first coming to the Word of Faith Movement, she has become critical of its teachings—at least the attitude that they sometimes seem to engender in some people—while remaining sympathetic to some of its principles or concepts. She does not consider herself to be a supporter of the movement to the extent that she once did, if at all. The key for her, and for many others who participated in this study, is the need to find a realistic balance and not take the idea of positive confession (or other teachings) to extremes.

Together the comments and experiences shared in this section offer a glimpse into the culture that is informed by the teaching of positive confession—from Russell not getting a flu shot, despite all the advertisers' and other people's insistence that "it's cold and flu season," to the experience of Charlene, another young woman I interviewed: she related to me that several years ago, when they were all quite a bit younger, some of her friends in the Word of Faith Movement would actually correct her speech in order to, as she saw it, "enlighten this person who is still stuck in a first church mentality."

Arlette's anecdote about the group who balked at singing a song in which they would be required to say that God has given them "strength to suffer" illustrated the movement's teaching: that through our spoken words (and unspoken thoughts) we actually create the circumstances of our lives—good or bad. Good, positive, godly circumstances and blessings occur as a result of Christians knowing that since they are in Christ, they have *power*, given to them as part of the contract they have with God. It only follows, then, that if you expect and believe that God only wants the best and the most pleasant and blessed life for you that is possible, you should speak only affirming words, words that appear to concur with God's words in the Bible, words that have the power to create happiness, a divine state of good health (including healing for the sick), and prosperity in any number of forms and definitions.

But there are other things that might be said about positive confession. To some people it might appear to be a thinly disguised form of magic, witchcraft, or superstition—a Christianized form, in that people claim as its basis their knowledge and "revelation" of spiritual law, but to critics this practice is magic or witchcraft nonetheless. It may sound like superstition in that many people are actually *afraid* that the mere act of speaking a negative word (regardless of whether it is actually the truth) to someone will create a correspondingly negative situation. This might appear to be no different from throwing salt over your shoulder or knocking on wood as a means of negating some form of imminent disaster that might result from having spoken a certain word or tempted fate in some way. It is not uncommon for people to use this notion of the power of confession in everyday situations, as when someone sneezes. Instead of saying "Bless you" or "Gesundheit," as is customary in our culture at large, they commonly would respond with "I curse that sneeze in Jesus' name!" Here they are signifying the belief and teaching that believers' "cursing" a symptom (sneezing) can relieve disease of its power to harm the individual. What makes this act an example of the use of confession is the use of the spoken word, especially when authorized with scripture and by the phrase "in Jesus' name," with the intention of averting some undesired or negative outcome, replacing it with a desired, positive one.

Still another use of positive confession I have personally observed and experienced many times over the years has to do with natural occurrences like those that commonly accompany the aging process. In the company of another couple who were friends of my wife and mine, I once commented in passing that I was beginning to lose my hair—I simply said that it was "thinning" on top—to which I received one of the customary Word of Faith responses, complete with an application of positive confession. They replied to my simple observation with "Oh, no, don't confess that. We're believing for you a full head of hair. You're *not* going to lose your hair, in Jesus' name!" So regardless of my own observation of my own body, my genetic heritage, and other evidence, they instructed me in the course of our conversation not to confess what was happening on top of my own head and "believe for" a full head of hair along with their prayers for me.

These are both examples of well-meaning people using words to counteract some perceived negative circumstance or even the natural, physiological processes of sneezing and hair loss. But they also illustrate the way this practice of only using positive confession and *never* making a negative confession is believed to have power to alter objective reality.

Positive confession may also be thought of in another way. The testimony service of many traditional Pentecostal congregations, for example, allows members of the congregation to communicate in a conventionalized and indirect way their needs, desires, challenges, problems, victories to the rest of the body. By framing these disclosures in terms of publicly offering testimony of God's goodness in a particular situation, people have a structured mechanism for letting others know what is going on in their lives.[1]

Positive confession may be thought of as another conventionalized form of religious speech that serves a function like that of the testimony: it is a ritual way of letting others know what one is "believing for" so that if they have the means to give it—if "God lays it on their heart to plant the seed" they can meet that need. By telling others what we are "believing for"—and confessing by faith that we already have it—we let them know what it is we want. If they have it and decide to give, then they can say that God directed them to do so. In this way, positive confession can be seen as a modality of religious expression by which the material desires of the believer are communicated to others and which spiritualizes the mere expression of the desire as well as the fulfillment of it through the acquisition of some object or another. One final example illustrates the point.

During the course of this research and writing, the Pastor at Faith Christian Center was given a Learjet by a businessman whom God had "laid it on his heart" to donate it. It was commonly known that the pastor wanted this jet because he constantly talked about it publicly and had even given it a name. Even visiting ministers talked about it (many of them already had jets of their own), and the jet was even mentioned in a local newspaper's story about the church in which they said that the pastor was believing God for and expected to receive a jet airplane. By constantly confessing and making known to all who would hear, eventually someone heard who could meet that confessed desire and say that God told him to do it so this man of God could do more for "the kingdom." The pastor's jet is one example of the type of material wealth to which members of the Word of Faith Movement aspire. Within this worldview, there is nothing too big for them to dream or for God to deliver to the faithful and those who would dare to stand on his Word.

Katia: "I just kept telling them 'You know, the time will come when I will have so much that you guys will not believe it,' because God is on my side!"

For some of Katia's compatriots from the former Soviet Union, the Faith Message and its teachings were not so radical but were more a continuation or extension of a type of religious teaching they had already been exposed to through contact with missionaries or evangelists even before emigrating. For them, the idea that God wanted Christians, "His children," to have financial and material prosperity in addition to making it into heaven was not a novel idea when they arrived in America or at Faith Christian Center. But for Katia, the situation was different, as she explains:

> My experience was totally different regarding prosperity. I was raised in a Pentecostal church family, a very traditional family, I should say. My parents were not poor. My dad . . . at the time when we were leaving, he had a company. He had a construction company over there, and he had 150 people employed. You know, so we are not poor. But the thing was the church . . . what they preached was also poverty. People that are Christians should live in poverty. So our family were—was kind of persecuted from the church, and my dad he would not, he was not loud about it. He believed in his heart that it's not right [that Christians should live in poverty], but he never taught us that it's not right. He was not loud about it in the family. So there was a lot of *confusion* to me. When I grew up, I think that's one of the things—I hated God and the church—that's one of the reasons why. I heard that people have to be poor, and I did not see any light in the church in that area, you know? *And I could not imagine myself being poor.* So when I got saved, and when I heard this message of faith, message of prosperity, it really shook me. First of all, I was open, but on the other side, I heard a lot of negative about it, you know? So I was not receiving—even though I was seeking, I was not receiving [accepting the teaching].
>
> And what I decided [was] that I have to study it for myself. Especially when I heard John Avanzini talk about prosperity—it blew my mind, I'm telling you! I thought "this man is crazy, or he is, like, you know, how do you say . . . about a man who's trying to make money on earth . . . ? [Interviewer: a "crook?"] Yeah, like some kind of crook, you know? That's what I thought! But, actually, I carefully studied the Word—I just read every scripture about prosperity and about Jesus. And I found that Jesus was not poor, you know? That he had so much money that Judas was stealing from him, and they didn't even notice! So, in order not to notice that someone is stealing from you, you gotta have a lot, you know?
>
> So I choose to stick with the Word. I was saved in a very traditional church. You know, over here in Sacramento. But it's Russian—it's Russian Pentecostal church, and it's very traditional. So I did not hear a message of prosperity down there, and that was the first time I heard it, like, on TV—John Avanzini speaking. So when I studied and found out that's true—that, you know, I could not accept *every-*

thing that he said at that time, but at least I knew that he was teaching the Word of God, you know? And my church would not accept
that, you know, they were against that.

But in my personal life, I started exercising that and I found
that it's working and even though, my parents right now they believe that Christians . . . they believe that it's a lot from God. You
know? Some people's lot [in life] to be poor, and some people it's
just . . . God ordered them to be rich or you don't have any money.
But I see that it's not a lot in life. I do not believe that every person—
every single person has to have millions. I'm not saying that—I do
not find that in the Word—but what I found in the Word is that
God brought us an abundant life. Not just *life* but an *abundant* life—
and abundant means that you have enough for yourself and to give
to others. And whatever it might be, I don't know, it might be different figures for different people.

And also I found that there are some people who are called to
bring money in the church. You know, that's their *calling*. So there is
difference between those two. So I believe in prosperity. I believe
that everyone, every child of God has the right to stand in faith for
his or her finances.

Katia refers to one of the classical Christian positions that Faith teachers
attribute to the ignorance of denominational teaching. It is in this respect that
they see themselves and their movement as at the vanguard of God's new
revelation to the Christian church. Katia says that in Ukraine because her family was not poor they experienced some degree of social sanctioning from other
church members, who believed that Christians should live lives of poverty, or
at least that they should not go about actively seeking wealth. It might be
interesting to ask how the Communist economic system—although anticapi-
talist and antireligious—produced the social and cultural context that informs
this teaching concerning the relationship of Christians to money in the former
Soviet Union. This attitude can be found in other Christian denominations
and in other regions of the world, but I wondered whether Communism turned
up the volume on the adage that "money is the root of all evil" as opposed to
what the scripture in fact reads: "the *love* of money is the root of all evil."
Although her parents still seem to hold to a more fatalistic philosophy about
financial prosperity—that God ordains some people to have material wealth
and others not to have it (to whatever degree)—Katia thinks that being a good
Christian and having money can and *do* go together. For her as a Christian,
money is not off limits. She explains:

I see that in my own personal life, you know. God has been prospering me tremendously—especially when I came to Faith Christian Center—because I hear the Word all the time, and when you hear the Word, when you're reminded of the Word, it begins to live in you. It's like . . . the environment that you put a person in, that's what the person's gonna talk, gonna live, gonna act upon, you know? and I like the environment at Faith Christian Center. Especially about prosperity. The pastor is loud, he is straight about it, he teaches the Word.

In my own experience . . . when I came to Faith Christian Center, I was in debt. I just moved down here to this part of this town, and I had a debt of six thousand dollars because I have been constantly going to school, and I could not work as much as I wanted to. And my car was not paid off also. So I had six thousand dollars in debt, my car wasn't paid off, I did not have *anything*, you know— but some clothes—that's all I had. And when I heard this message preached—being preached, you know—I started exercising upon it. And I remember when Creflo Dollar came over and he preached about prosperity, and at that time I decided that—I had two hundred dollars that I'd just made, and I decided I'm gonna just give those monies away, you know?

So I just came and I put that in the offering and after that, I'm telling you, the breakthrough came! Within, like, six months my debt had been paid off, my car has been paid off. And within nine months I bought a house. And this is my second year at Faith Christian Center—I'm buying my third home! I'm not kidding you. My first home is almost paid off! So, I'm telling you, I can testify and testify how God blessed me, and I went through hard times.

I have to say, in the beginning, when I gave those monies away, I did not see the return for, like, maybe five months, and I've been through hell. But every morning I would get up and I would just praise God for the finances. And I was just testifying [telling others]. I did not see it, *but all of my friends knew that I will have a house, it will be paid off within a short time.* And some did not believe because I did not have *anything* at that time, not even a car, you know? And I was in debt, and they were laughing at me, but I just kept telling them, "you know, the time will come when I will have so much that you guys will not believe it because God is on my side." He is working on my side, and I have the Word of God to stand upon. And I stood, and I went through *horrible* times when I did not have a *dol-*

lar, and a dollar was so much money to me that I was, like [groaning] . . . a lot of money. But because God's Word is true, and because I *stood* fast, I can testify of his mercy.

I wanted to know if she thought all she had achieved in the United States would have been possible in Ukraine (becoming a real estate agent and purchasing three houses), with or without the Word of Faith movement's teaching about prosperity. She replied that she didn't really know that for sure. She did say, however, that although there are obviously more opportunities for financial prosperity (or upward mobility) in the United States, she is confident that when one *applies the teachings* and *believes that it is God's will* for one to do so, one can prosper financially in whichever country one happens to be living. Finally, I wanted her to explain to me why she thought she was prospering, to "sum it up." She replied:

> Because the Word of God gives us a base—it says that Jesus did not just bring life, he brought *abundant* life, and, like in other scripture it says "I want you to . . ." [trying to remember the exact reference, Timothy 2] it says that I want you to live in peace and not to beg anyone else around you, but *be a blessing to others*—that's my interpretation of it, you know? be a blessing to others and give to others.
> And that's the way I see abundance—that it's not just having enough or barely enough for yourself, it's the stage where you can be a blessing to others, and that was my prayer—it's not just for me, but I was praying "God, make me a channel of your blessings. Make me a channel to other people. So we can reach this world with the gospel of Christ." And I believe because of it I'm blessed, and I will be blessed even more—you'll hear it on the TV one day! [She laughs]

The purpose or *reason* given by Katia for prosperity—to have enough so that one can be a blessing to others—is one of the most important and overlooked points about the teaching on prosperity. From the outside looking in, it is easy to see this as little more than rampant, vulgar materialism. It may appear that people are being encouraged to amass wealth, or that the promise of wealth is being set before those whose socioeconomic origins and resources place them the furthest from access to it. But there is more to the teaching of prosperity than mere money-grubbing. That would be too simplistic an appraisal. The people are being taught that it is God's desire to "prosper" them and meet their financial needs in order to make them channels of those same financial blessings toward those who are still in need.

This may appear to be a paradox the Word of Faith Movement's philosophy with respect to the distribution and redistribution of material wealth, but in reality it is consistent with the values underlying the Faith Message. On one hand, if individuals are *not* prospering, it is assumed to be their own fault in some way, so that, at least implicitly, the victims are being blamed for their situation. They may be in sin, lacking faith, or they may simply be ignorant and in need of the Faith Message's teaching that it is God's will for believers to be financially prosperous to be able to claim that prosperity for themselves. But during offerings, for example, the pastor frequently asks those without money to give to raise their hands. Other members of the congregation are then encouraged to look around for those whose hands are raised, and then to go place money into those outstretched hands. So the ethic of acquiring wealth is coupled with the teaching that God blesses in order to make believers responsible for the poor and the less fortunate until they learn to claim prosperity for themselves. This is not such a foreign concept in the history of the Christian church, but critics and outsiders often miss this point when discussing the movement's emphasis on material wealth. This ethic is also at the heart of the divine health and healing part of the teaching: the abundant life Christ came to bring those who would accept him is expressed as "God can do more with us (use us) more when we are physically healthy and full of energy than when we are sick and our strength is sapped by disease." So the emphasis is again on how one can serve others through the gifts of prosperity bestowed upon Christians as their heritage as being in Christ.

But there is still a part of the Faith Message's teaching concerning prosperity that causes distress and great concern for those attempting to believe and practice it in their own lives. For example, the part of the teaching which emphasizes what is known as the "seed-time and harvest" principle, that is, whenever someone gives (whether in an offering at church or directly to another person) they are actually planting financial seeds from which they will later be able to reap the harvest of financial blessings in kind. The evangelist Oral Roberts is generally credited with having contributed this element, known as "seed-faith," to the Faith Message. The parable of Jesus in Matthew 4, which speaks of the sower sowing seeds that produced a thirty-, a sixty-, or a hundredfold return, provides the scriptural basis for this point of doctrine. However, this interpretation can be problematic. Believers who sow financial "seeds" come to expect a direct, correlative return—in financial form—as a result. Some people give money, wait for the return on their "investment," and end up being disappointed when it does not appear to come to them when and how they expect it. According to the Faith Message, not only has the act of giving offerings been redefined as an act of personal devotion to God, one that allows the work of spreading the gospel and building the church to continue, but also giving is seen as an investment that is virtually guaranteed to yield tangible, material returns for the believer.

The teaching that giving money—especially tithing on a regular, consistent basis—will result in financial prosperity can place believers in a very precarious position, threatening their ability to actually realize the promise of financial abundance while frightening them with the possibility of losing what they have due to God's wrath or the withdrawal of his protection. One of the people who participated in this study offered some comments that graphically illustrated the sense of insecurity the movement can engender in its members.

Fran is a professional woman. She is African American, in her mid-thirties, unmarried, and an executive in a national retail chain. She is a homeowner and at the time of our interview had an annual income of more than $50,000. She had the following response to my reading of a passage from one of the most renowned of today's Faith teachers on the issue of prosperity:

> I tell you honestly, when it's prosperity, that's something—well, I've got to work on that one. Because that one I don't really believe yet—it's not that I don't believe it, it's just . . . I haven't seen the manifestation of prosperity yet.
>
> I think what he's meaning there is that prosperity is a part of faith. And that if you have faith and apply the principles that he talks about in tithing and giving, that you will receive the blessings of God. But I've done those and I haven't per se seen them. You know, that one's kinda hard because I could stand in faith for things that are not financial quicker than I can stand for things that are financial. And I don't—I haven't gotten why that is yet. Because I've given several times at church to the over-and-above situation and I have yet to get, like—you know—the hundredfold or the tenfold back.

Elaborating on what she meant by the "over-and-above" situation, she went on to explain:

> Five years ago they were asking for a thousand dollars, so I gave a thousand dollars. And I don't know if you can say that this house is part of that prosperity, but I don't think it is because I'm paying monthly on it. I didn't get a lump sum like they say you're supposed to get, you know. And they say if you sow seed—if you sow finances—that's what you get back! Well, I haven't gotten that back, you know? If I put a thousand dollars in, I should be able to get ten thousand

back, or something—I haven't even gotten *two* thousand back, you know what I'm saying? And, to me, your taxes—that's not part of the overflow cause that's what you paid into.

And then, I gave five hundred dollars one time, and then recently I gave another thousand, and it's like "well, when am I gonna get my *money?!*" You know, I sowed into—I'm trying to believe the Word. I sow—and then I thought, "Well, maybe it's because I don't pay my tithes consistently, you know?" So maybe that's why I'm not receiving the blessings because I'm not applying the principles— I'm not doing what God tells me to do in order for me to get it. But then I think to myself "Well, God, I do almost everything else right, you know. Why are you being such a stickler on this part, but you bless me faith-wise on other things. You know that I didn't get killed that time, and I wasn't perfect then. So why is this money issue so hard to see the manifestation? So, I haven't gotten that one yet.

I wanted her to explain the effect of this seeming inconsistency between belief and practice and the actual result she has experienced. I asked her how she felt that the ministers in her church (and the movement in general) are telling her one thing—that she should *expect* a certain thing, a certain type and form of "return" on her giving—and the reality that she doesn't feel like she's getting it. She replied:

Well, sometimes it makes me hesitate to give. But then I feel "Well, if I don't give, then I'm not standing in faith. So that's one that I fight in my mind all the time. Because I wanna give in faith and I wanna believe in faith, but then I don't ever see the return, so then it makes me not wanna give again. But, then, the pastor will talk about something and makes you kinda feel bad that you want—that you *have to* give. So I kinda give begrudgingly. And maybe that's bad because [the Bible] says don't give begrudgingly! So maybe that's hindering me from getting my blessing. Because I'm giving begrudgingly. But I wouldn't give begrudgingly if I saw the fruits of what I've given in the past, you know? Or even when you give to someone. I've sowed into people and I haven't gotten that back. But then maybe sometimes you don't get back money, maybe you get back peace of mind or something. Or maybe the blessings that the Lord has given my family is [the result of] my financial blessing. And that's fine, but they shouldn't say if you sow money, you get back money. They should just say "You sow and then God gives you different ways," you know?

Then she summed up her thoughts on the overall prosperity teaching as she understood and had experienced it:

I think it's good, but I think that area to me the church doesn't understand. Because I don't see nobody really prospering at church. I mean, only one I see is pastors [prospering]! All these people are giving at church, but we don't have millionaires! Why—we should have *millionaires!* But I think that's a hard one for everybody to grasp. 'Cause if it wasn't, then he [the pastor] wouldn't be having such a hard time getting [money] from people! You know, they don't wanna give it up because they don't never see nothing coming back maybe!

[Interviewer: Then the ministers wouldn't have to talk about it so much?]

Right! Because we have to live. I mean, maybe that's a *true* test of our faith because we don't wanna give up money 'cause we know we have to pay bills and live off of that. But if we give that up then we'll be out on the street. But . . . I guess if we had true faith, then we would believe God and it would be okay, you know? But that's a hard one, I think—not just for me, but for people in general.

I think I struggle in giving because I haven't seen the manifestations. I mean, through faith in *other* areas I've seen manifestations. So it makes me step out in faith quickly, *quicker* in those instances than in money issues. Like, I could believe and pray for, a new car or something—and that's dealing with money too, but that's not actually, physical money, that's money in another form. And I could pray, believe for, that rather than actual *money in my hand.* And I don't understand that. Or like, recently, I had paid a thousand dollars for church, and then I was trying to stand in faith and believe God. And then it I was getting to where I needed *money,* you know what I'm saying? I was like "Oh, no!" you know, I was trying to believe God, and I said "See, with that thousand dollars I could've paid this bill, and this bill, and this bill." Then I said "Well, Father God, you know my situation; when is the money going to come?"

And then I waited and waited. And I have some bonds; I cashed them in and got the money that I needed! And I thought, "Well, that's not believing in faith." But I waited, and waited—I mean, I don't know how long I was supposed to wait! Was I supposed to wait 'til I get out on the street? Or maybe I wasn't stretching myself because I knew I had those certificates that I could cash in. So maybe I haven't been desperate enough yet or something. But to me, why should you have to be *desperate* in order for [God] to bring it to you? You know, bring what you've already given, that you're just waiting for your manifestation. I don't think you have to be that desperate, to me, but seems like we're always desperate and then that's when he brings it. But he doesn't do other things like that.

I asked if she could name anyone she considered to be prosperous. She answered:

Like I said, I don't know nobody! I mean, the people that I know none of them are sitting high with no cares or nothin'. I don't wanna name people, but I mean like [name], my friend, and you guys are my friends—none of us are really sitting pretty or—like Sister [name]. I'm thinking "Now, Sister [name], she applies *all* the principles. You know, the people that apply all the principles, they ain't even prosperous. I'm thinking "What is goin' on here?" See, I don't understand stuff like that.

I asked her what she thought is the *purpose* of prosperity. Why is that something we should even be concerned about? Why is that important? She replied:

I think it's important because I think there're more people *outside* of the church that are prosperous than we are. And I think that if we're living the life of Christ, or living an upright life, then we should have just as—at least equal to, or more than what the people who ain't' doing right have. You know, one day I was on a conference call at work. And we had 20 people on there, everyone was connected up together. And there was this guy that's the marketing manager, and the big man in [her company's headquarters] said, "Well, how are sales?" and he said, "Oh, they're not doing good." And this man— it shocked me when he said this—he said, "Well, you gotta pay your tithes, you know. 'Cause that works." And this man doesn't go to church at all! And I was shocked because I know—I thought those other 19 people didn't know what he was talkin' 'bout. I thought but he don't even go to church—I mean, he ain't *into* the church—but he knows that when he pay tithes something happens! And I thought "God, people that ain't even saved are doing the principles of God, and *they're* prospering, so why can't *I* prosper when I'm do- ing, supposedly, right?"

I'm not perfect . . . I mean, I lose it, or I may not go to church every three weeks or something like that, or I get frustrated and then I go off on the deep end, but I mean most of the time I try to do right. But why isn't prosperity working for me? I don't understand.

Ambivalence, confusion, frustration, and even hurt and disillusionment seem to ring through in Fran's comments. But it sounds as though she blames herself—her lack of *understanding* seems to her to be at least some of the cause of her failure to experience the great financial prosperity promised by those who teach the Faith Message. This is a person who is a professional, who makes an excellent living (more than some of the married couples I interviewed), but because of the way the Faith Message has shaped her expectations of how the principles of prosperity work, she is feeling frustrated and just seems not to understand the whole thing. Asked to identify who really is prospering, she says that most of those she sees around her are *not* prospering financially, and that they are struggling just like she is. There was, however, one person she thought was prosperous based on outward appearances: clothing, grooming, car, type of house, and so on. But she also said that she thought the woman seemed to be "troubled."

During the course of our discussion, she said that she thought this woman was not prospering "on the inside." This could just be an instance of sour grapes. Perhaps, however, in the absence of the types of conspicuous displays of wealth like the Rolls Royces and Learjets that so many of the Faith teachers have defined as necessities now, people in the movement must fall back on the recognition of other types of prosperity to which they actually do have access.

Given the movement's penchant for creatively redefining the meanings of words, thereby making them reality-constructing, power-filled confessions, the use of the word "finances" should not be overlooked (it was the First Annual *Finance* Convention that opened chapter 1 of this book). For people in the Word of Faith Movement, money is frequently referred to in a way that seems to elevate its status and, by extension, their own relationship to it. Poor people, those under the curse of poverty or who have a "poverty mentality," lack *money* (or are characterized as "low-income"). Wealthy people, who are blessed or who have a "prosperity mentality," possess and manage *finances*, which calls to mind the idea of *capital*, for investment and other forms of manipulation in the marketplace. So even in the very words chosen to talk about it, the attitude and value placed on money, and the preferred relationship to it, can be seen as central to the Faith Message.

Several people, when asked whether they felt they were prosperous, answered in the affirmative. They also argued that there are more ways to measure prosperity than in terms of finances, which seems to be the dominant unit of measurement in the larger society and is reflected in the Word of Faith Movement's teaching. One woman said that although she may not yet be as financially prosperous as she believed she would someday be, she was at present "prosper-*ing*," meaning that she was in the *process of becoming* prosperous. This way of reckoning is a departure from the sharp dichotomy commonly (if unintentionally) portrayed in the movement. It might also be seen as a way of negotiating the disparity between the ideal and the everyday reality of her life and the lives of many other believers.

Living the Faith Message

Let us consider how members integrate the whole of the Faith Message into some of the most mundane aspects of their daily lives. Asked how many times per day she did something "religious" in addition to prayer, positive confession, or anything she (or I) might call practicing her religion, Cassandra had the following to say.

> I don't know how many times. I start off in the morning with that, but one thing I used to do [is] you know how you set aside that certain time for [prayer]—you know, "I'm going to pray 30 minutes." But I've learned as I've grown that prayer is talking to God *throughout* the day. And I now feel free to do that, whereas before I felt like there's just this thing, you know, you talk to him before you leave the house and you don't really talk anymore.
>
> Growing up [I thought] that God was that Father, that Almighty— he was God before he was Father. And now that I see him as Father and *then* God, it makes a bit of a difference. It's made a difference for me. I can talk to my *Father* anytime I want to! And I find myself doing that throughout the day: "Okay, Father, what's going on here?" You know, just little stuff like that. To me that's praying. Because praying is just talking to God. And then there's that quiet time when I feel like I need to just listen, and then I write down stuff that I believe that God is saying to me. And I usually start off, you know, in the morning doing that, but not with the big ritual . . . prayer. I'd say on a daily basis, just throughout the day. So I couldn't put a time, a number of times . . . I guess it's just so much a part of me, I don't really think about it much.

Sometimes I do, and sometimes I don't [say a blessing over my food when I eat]. That varies. I'm trying to get to where I'm doing it more often—giving thanks to God for [the food]. But . . . I don't do it as often as I should. Or often as I'd like to. No, let me say often as I *should. God knows I'm thankful* whether I'm bowing my head and saying it or not. I'm thankful. I . . . well, let me just say I bow my head and pray when I want to! [laughing] Or when I think about it I do it sometimes, sometimes I don't.

[Interviewer: It doesn't have to be separate, set-aside moment?]

No, it's not a whole separate [moment]. As you grow you learn to *creatively incorporate* the Word of God in your own life, the way it fits into *your* life. There's not one way of talking to God. There's not one way of applying God's Word. There's not one way of under-standing His Word. Because I think we understand it . . . based on our own *experiences.*

Cassandra also shared with me how in the course of her day as a case worker, going into the houses of people who have children in foster care, she constantly and almost seamlessly blends aspects of the Faith Message with her professional duties. For example, she shared that recently, before entering the house of a particularly contentious and troublesome client, she stopped to pray and to visualize the outcome of the interaction as being positive and working out in the best interest of the child whose advocate she sees herself as. The fact that she does not maintain a set-aside, ritualized, ceremonial time of prayer, choosing rather to "talk to God all through the day," and her comment that she believes that God knows she's thankful, whether she's bowing her head and saying it or not, shows how people creatively incorporate religion ("the Word of God," as Cassandra put it) into their lives.

Another instance of creatively incorporating faith into everyday situations came from Russell.

I thought I heard Russell say in passing that he and his wife only purchase red vehicles. Thinking I had misheard him, I asked him to repeat what he had said and, please, to elaborate on it. He said they also have personalized license plates with scriptures on them:

But [for] all of our vehicles, now we're buying red because of the blood [of Christ]. We're putting on personal license plates and red vehicles for the blood. The license plate number on the truck says GODZ 4 US. God's for us. The license plate on the van is PRAZ 2 HM, which is "Praise to Him." Praise to him. That's on the van.

[Interviewer: So all of your vehicles will now be red from now on?]

Yep. With scripture license plates. With scripture license plates so . . . when people follow us, whether it's a police officer on the freeway or whether it's just a car. In fact, I've driven into gas stations that say "pay first" and they looked at my license plate and said "Don't worry about it. Just pump it." That's favor with being a Christian. God allows us to receive favor. But I pray about favor all the time. I operate in favor, and the favor of God is all around us. And the favor of God is not only around us but it's in us and it affects those, those that we come in contact with. And people are blessed because of where *we* work. People are blessed *because of who we are.* And it's God in us.

We just speak out what the Bible teaches about giving. We operate the principles. *And because we operate the principles, we receive the blessings.*

Certainly the basis for Russell's decision to purchase only red vehicles will not be found explicitly taught in the Bible. But it is a way he and his wife have chosen to take a mass-produced, mundane item and transform it into a part of their religious practice: "witnessing." For evangelical Christians, no opportunity should be wasted in which one can share the gospel and potentially "lead [non-Christians] to the Lord." The sign next to the front door of Russell's house, remember, announced to guests "As for me and my house, we will serve the Lord." It was another part of this family fulfilling the duty that evangelicals believe is theirs: to make the whole world (or as many as possible) into Christians before the imminent return of Christ. It is interesting and instructive to see these ideals translated into practice in the form of buying a certain color vehicle and having scripturally meaningful encoded, "vanity" license plates (which are very common with members of the Word of Faith Movement, as they probably are with other evangelicals), especially when the car is a culturally understood status symbol like a Mercedes or Cadillac. The car and the license plates become yet another way of confessing and testifying (signifying) prosperity and making the direct conceptual linkage between one's faith and one's possession of the status symbol.

A final example, also involving an automobile, further illustrates the practice of imbuing mundane objects or situations with spiritual significance. Fran shared a humorous experience with me as a specific instance when she applied positive confession:

Actually two, I'll give you two! There was one time I was over [at] a boyfriend's house (which I shouldn't have been). I was over [at] a boyfriend's house that my mom and dad didn't like 'cause he was older, he was like 10 years older, and I went to visit him and while I was visiting him, my car got stolen! Because he lived next to a store and the people robbed the store, and out of all of the apartment complexes the people stole my car! [Interviewer: To be the getaway car?] Yes! So when I got done visiting him, I went out and I said, "Now, I know I left my car here"—you know, walking around. And this is a shame, this is why you shouldn't be with people you shouldn't be with: 'cause he was not worried about my car being stolen. He was not worried at all! So, I went home and told my mom that my car got stolen. And, uh . . . they was mad 'cause, you know, I was over there! *But for seven days I prayed that my car would come back to me.* And at work—I told them at work that my car had got stolen, and they said "Oh, you need to put in, uh, you know, on your insurance that your car—" and I said, "No, I'm not gonna do that. I am praying"—every night after work I would come home and pray for at least an hour. And I found scriptures and I prayed those specific scriptures every night. *And then every time somebody at work, or my mom, would say something—like, they'd say "Ooh, you're not gonna get your—" I'd say "No, yes, I"*— I'd pray those actual scriptures *against* what they were saying. *And in seven days my car came back.* They found my—no, they called my dad, called our home and told them that they had found my car, that it was in a parking lot, like, up in Auburn. And it had a full tank of gas, and it wasn't even broken!

So all we had to do was go up there and get it

[Interviewer: How'd they get in? Did they—did you have—was it unlocked?]

It was like a car that you could just pop the thing and just go in. And it came back and I was so excited! 'Cause—I mean, but—I *applied* the Word of God and I stood on it and I didn't waver and didn't allow negativity to come in—

[Interviewer: From the other people?]

Right.

[Interviewer: Saying that you're not gonna get it back or you should put in a—what would have happened if you had, if—in your mind—you had filed an insurance claim?]

I know that there are some instances where you should do that, but I think to me I was testing my faith. Because I didn't know what else to do. And so I said "Well, I'm just gonna try it." And it worked. But there's other instances where I've done other things— gone to the hospital or whatever you need to do, but in that instance I don't know why I stood in faith. For that particular instance, maybe I just felt that it would happen and it did, you know?

In this example, Fran was able to use the teachings in the Faith Message concerning positive confession, going to the Bible for specific scriptures to "pray against" the negative words the people around her were *saying* in the situation.

This chapter has been concerned with members of the Word of Faith Movement struggling to "work out their own salvation"—to make sense of, and implement, their own, practical understanding of the Faith Message they are being taught in their local church. Whether they were discussing their use of the principle of "knowing who you are in Christ," the practice of positive confession, or the promise of abundant life and prosperity that is held out as what God wills for Christians, together their comments and insights help show us that making meaning in terms of religious doctrine is indeed done through the process of living everyday life.

From the point of view of what we have come to think of as traditional Christian beliefs and practices, one might not expect to hear someone say that he and his wife only purchase red vehicles "because of the blood [of Christ]" symbolized in the color of a simple car or van. In this way driving (or parking, or even possessing) the vehicle with the special plates becomes a form of religious practice and another of the ways in which people imbue profane objects (and situations) with sacred significance. Through the assemblage of these everyday items into a medium for the sacred, these everyday theologians are creatively reproducing religion in the most mundane locations and in interactions with people that are not bounded by the constraints or proscriptions of institutionalized forms of religion. They may have heard the Faith Message in their church, but the ways they have found to express its meanings to those outside the church are largely matters of creativity and necessity.

3

Faith Christian Center

To whomsoever much is given, of him shall be much required:
And to whom men have committed much, of him they will ask the
more.

—Luke 12:48

The first beats of the drum, amplified by the state-of-the-art sound
system, set the heart pounding with excitement, anticipation, expec-
tancy. Three attractive young African American women—barefoot
and wearing black leotards and ethnic-print sarong-type skirts—
dance slowly, lyrically down the center aisle, drawing wide, sweeping
arcs with the silver and gold fans in their hands. Moving together,
they reach their place on the stairs at the front of the sanctuary and
smile welcomingly as they turn to face the audience. From the three
main aisles they are followed by people of many racial backgrounds,
costumed to represent various nations of our global village. Here a
teenage African American male is dressed as a Russian cossack;
there a middle-aged, olive-skinned woman wears a long Hawaiian
dress and lei, a crown of flowers encircling her head. There is an
American cowboy character and a woman dressed as a Native American, with a buckskin dress, hair parted down the middle into two
braids, and a headband with a feather in back. Still another woman
wears what appears to be a synthesis of Italian and Spanish cos-
tume, of white, green, and red, with a black lace mantilla and casta-
nets in her hands. These also take their places along the front of the

sanctuary and keep time as they await the next wave in this parade. There are laughing children skipping down the aisle, single file, performing a popular dance step, "the running-man;" hip-hop youth dancers in black T-shirts, baggy pants, and sneakers; a group of women of various ages and races waving long ribbons on sticks, and tall flag bearers with gold-sequined banners in rich purple, blue, or red velvet reading "Jesus" and "Overcomer" held high above the heads of the congregation.

Many in the audience are on their feet applauding or cheering as each part of the event unfolds in its turn. This is an exciting moment on an early Sunday morning. It is a time of inter-national and inter-ethnic appreciation, celebration, and universal Christian love. Accompanying all this pageantry is the song "Praise the Lord, Everybody," and the maps and flags of a parade of world nations are projected, one after the other, onto two large video monitors located on either side of the platform. But this is just the beginning of this multimedia event, a veritable "love-a-thon," all in the name of racial reconciliation and of defeating the claim that eleven o'clock on Sunday morning is America's most segregated hour of the week.

Today is this month's fourth Sunday, or Multicultural Sunday, the day on which each member of the congregation has been instructed by the pastor to reach out to someone outside his or her own racial/ethnic group and invite them to come and worship together in unity at Faith Christian Center, the "church without walls." That is, it is the church without the walls of prejudice, bigotry, ignorance, and hatred that have kept Christians separated for generations. This morning's multicultural appreciation program is one of many programs regularly sponsored and presented by this dynamic church in its effort to remain relevant and to attract members from a wide variety of backgrounds. Since the early 1990s, racial reconciliation and multiculturalism have been part of an ongoing discourse among evangelical Christians across the country. This local church's program encouraging awareness and appreciation across boundaries of race and ethnicity—in the context of the Word of Faith Movement's teachings on prosperity—is a demonstration of the way the movement shares some concerns with other evangelical congregations while it is very distinct in others.

We can gain entrance to the culture within the Word of Faith Movement by examining one of its member congregations: Faith Christian Center in Sacramento, California. At this congregation the Faith Message is taught to literally thousands of people each week through worship services, Bible studies, and the weekly television broadcast. This church is therefore a major site on the map of the Word of Faith Movement in northern California.

In what ways does the Faith Message inform the culture in this local church? How do the members of this church use the specifics of their move-ment's doctrine to distinguish themselves from the denominational churches, or what they refer to as the "first church"? What elements of social control and regulation can be seen at work here in this congregation? How do the Word of Faith Movement and this particular congregation articulate some of the aspects of wider dialogues found in contemporary American evangelicalism?

Faith Christian Center, Sacramento, California

The neighborhood in which Faith Christian Center[1] is located is not an eco-nomically prosperous one, according to census data (1990). The median house-hold income in 1989 was reported to be $14,290 within this census tract, compared to the median household income of $32,297 for the entire metro-politan area.[2] Similarly, in the area in which the church is located, the per-centage of people who are high school graduates or higher (but not having a bachelor's degree) is 52.3 percent; those with bachelor's degrees or higher make up only 2.8 percent. For the overall metropolitan area, the same categories yield percentages of 59 percent and 23 percent, respectively. Finally, the median housing value in the area where the church is located was reported at $63,700, compared to $129,000 for the overall metropolitan area. On two of these three indicators, figures for the immediate census tract where the church is located were less than half those representing the overall metropolitan area of which this neighborhood is part.

Sacramento's pattern of expansion and development is reflected in the church's gradual, yet steady, expansion since the early 1980s. In addition to the main church building (completed in 1995) and another building one block away that serves as an annex and houses the children's school, several sur-rounding apartment complexes and houses have also been acquired by the church. Many of the houses that sat on the blocks immediately surrounding the church were razed long ago to make way for this new main church building. Adjoining the new building is the former main church building, now used and referred to as "the chapel." The acquisition of property and expansion of the real holdings of Faith has long been, and continues to be, a central feature of the church's presence in the neighborhood, prompting some of the ministry's opponents to speak of it as "the church that *ate* North Sacramento." According to public records, reported in a recent article in the local independent news-paper, the pastor and the church own together more than 30 pieces of property, most of it in the immediate area surrounding the church. The same article reported that the church's total assets are approximately $18 million, and according to a quarterly report issued to members, the church took in $3.5 million in tithes and offerings alone for the year 1997. The church staff includes 50 paid employees, and an unknown number of unpaid workers regularly volunteer their services through more than 120 separate ministries that the church offers to its members and to the community.[3]

One of those ministries is the Overcomers' Program, the county's largest—and reportedly most successful—drug rehabilitation program. With approximately 100 clients, the Overcomers' Program is a residential program, and participants, both male and female, live in separate same-sex housing owned by the church. Fraternization with the opposite sex is strictly forbidden and is grounds for immediate dismissal. Participants in the program must attend Bible studies and all services, and as a group they all sit together in the same area in the sanctuary. Some of them also participate as workers in various ministries in the church.

The pastor and founder of this ministry, an African American in his early fifties, holds no political office but wields a degree of power and influence in the affairs of the city. He is leader of one of the largest and fastest-growing congregations in town, with a self-reported membership in excess of 8,000 people that began just over 20 years ago as a Bible study with fewer than 20 members. As the senior pastor of this dynamic, "on the move" congregation, he has nurtured this organization along to its present position as an important institutional base for evangelical Christianity, as well as one of the most prominent Word of Faith Ministries in northern California. The profile of this church and the movement in northern California has been raised even more since the ministry took to the television airwaves in the early 1990s. The presence of several large television cameras operated by technicians in headphones, and at various times directed into the faces of congregants in the worship services (as well as the pastor's repeated references to "those of you in the television audience"), serve to remind the congregation that the aim of this ministry and its message extend beyond those sitting in the sanctuary. During campaign seasons, prominent conservative candidates have been known to stop by and deliver an appropriately tailored version of their platform and campaign promises. Members of the church's Political Action Committee routinely draw up and distribute to members a brochure suggesting how they should vote on issues deemed important by or to the church, to the family, or to the maintenance of evangelical, conservative, Christian values in public policy. The leadership at Faith Christian Center has no intention of keeping church and state separate or of being left out of discussions of what is best for Sacramento and all of its citizens, Christian or otherwise. The pastor is frequently heard to say that his and the church's goal is to "take the city, the state, the country, and the world for Jesus."

The Culture inside the Ministry

Faith Christian Center is a very demanding ministry. One does not just come to church once a week, on Sunday mornings, and have no job in the ministry. So-called pew-warmers—those members who attend church but who are otherwise inactive—are not highly valued here. Members are taught that according to the Bible, "to whom much is given, much is required." Much is certainly required of Faith's members for all that is given to them in terms of the many programs, social activities, outreaches, special performances, opportunities for fellowship, and, of course, the dynamic, charismatic, energetic, and frequently entertaining pastor in whose image this church has been made. He demands the members' full participation and unwavering support—the almost absolute devotion of their time, attention, labor, and money—and apparently feels no compunction in making such demands.

Crossing Symbolic Boundaries: Becoming a Member of the Congregation

Those who join a new church (just as with any other type of organization or group) must go through a process of acculturation or socialization by which they learn the details of the distinctive culture at work within this new social entity. Whether the organization or group has formal structures to handle this essential task or whether it is accomplished informally, it is still necessary, and it can enable inclusion to occur as efficiently and quickly as possible. This organizational imperative is even more pressing in the context of a ministry whose outreach programs are extensive and through whose doors on a weekly basis come thousands of people, many of whom pledge their desire to become members of the congregation in the altar call held at the end of each service. Like many other ministries Faith Christian Center has an institutionalized means of socializing these newcomers: the New Membership Class.

Members of Faith Christian Center, and other Word of Faith Movement churches like it, commonly refer to their churches as "Word" churches. It is a way of distinguishing themselves from traditional denominational churches or other types of independent churches. The designation *Word church* means to them that a church's minister specializes in teaching, as opposed to preaching, what the Bible "really" says, the implication being that other churches do not do this. Movement members also refer to their churches as "teaching ministries." To the extent that this objective is to be realized, it becomes very important for all those who would become members to attend what are known as New Membership Classes. In these classes, those who have raised their hands, signifying their acceptance of the invitation to membership extended in the altar call, are led through the church's formal Statement of Beliefs and Teachings. Over a 10-week term (with rolling enrollment), they are taught that each point on the statement is scriptural and comes directly from the Bible. Students are then led to those scriptures and instructed to write them down for future reference. Along with identifying the scriptural reference for each point in the Statement, the teacher of that day's lesson expounds upon the meaning of the passages and gives examples from their own experience. The teacher, usually a seasoned volunteer from the congregation, may also answer questions from the students, although theological dialogue or debate is discouraged. Along with the pastor's weekly message or Bible study, these classes are one of the primary settings in which potential new members are introduced to the local church's officially recognized meanings of the Faith Message.

The New Membership classes are held at various times during the week: Wednesday nights before Bible study and Sunday mornings between services; and sometimes there are special accelerated courses in which one can cover the entire 10 weeks' worth of lessons in one weekend. Other churches may have no such classes at all or may condense their new members' orientation to a few hours, requiring new members to appear only once. At Faith potential members are each given a small card on the day they respond to the invitation at the end of each service. On this card are spaces for the date and the initials of the teacher of each of the 10 lessons. Since the classes are always in session, one can just pick up in the middle and wait until the beginning of the sequence starts again to make up any that have been missed. There is no set time frame by which one must have completed one's New Membership classes—that is, unless one wants to work in the ministry, which everyone is encouraged to do. One who has not completed these classes is not considered a full member of the congregation and thus not qualified, according to the rules, to work in the church.

In their interactions with others, particularly official members, prospective members receive frequent hints and cues to complete this series of classes. They are constantly made aware that they cannot fully participate in the workings or the governance of the church (occupying a leadership position, for example) until they have committed to and completed this course of study.

They are not yet formally part of the community until they have completed these classes. Admission to the community, crossing the boundary from outsider to insider, depends on this.

It is also in the New Membership classes that the prospective member becomes socialized to (among a host of other things) the ways the Word of Faith Movement's emphasis on teaching is expressed in the weekly sermon, Bible study, or any other time of doctrinal instruction. One learns what to expect from the speakers or teachers and how one will be addressed as part of the congregation, even as one learns the specifics of the doctrine. Prospective members also learn what will be expected of them as members of the congregation. For example, they learn that they are expected to have a Bible (preferably the King James translation) and to bring it to church with them, along with a writing implement and a notepad of some sort to take notes during the message.[4] These notes are then to be used as part of the individual's personal prayer and Bible study time during the following week. If one does not already know, this teaches that one is expected to spend personal time studying the Bible and in prayer.

In these New Membership classes, prospective members are exposed to the formula, or model, for how the Bible is taught to lay people in the Word of Faith churches. Implicitly, and by example in these classes, they are taught that the speaker makes a claim that then must be proved (or refuted) by textual evidence found in scripture. Again, prospective members are admonished to keep their own Bibles with them at all times (whether at church, on the job, or in public, for the purpose of witnessing or just personal study). They are told to read along with the instructor, writing down the scriptural references as they move through the day's lesson. They are encouraged to personalize many of the things they read in the Bible by writing their own names in places of words like ye, thou, and so on. When, for example, they read a line of scripture like "Beloved, I wish above all things that thou mayest prosper and be in health even as thy soul prospereth," it is a standard part of the belief system to think of that sentence as God speaking directly to each of them individually. As an act of their faith they should write their names in place of the second person pronouns. These classes help ease the prospective members into the routine they will encounter during the sermons in Word of Faith Movement churches.

At the end of those 10 weeks, having their completed attendance card in hand, the prospective new member is then called forward at one of the designated evening services and presented to the rest of the congregation, which responds with thunderous applause. New members are then given the "right hand of fellowship" and welcomed into the ministry. They are presented to the congregation specifically as those who have finished their New Membership classes and, as such, are to be fully recognized as members of the church— with all the rights and privileges of the full member. Veterans are encouraged to file past these new members and shake their hands, beginning with the pastor and his wife, followed by the ministerial staff, and then the congregation at large. This process may vary in other Word of Faith Movement churches, but regardless of the specifics of the ritual by which they are "fellowshipped in" (meaning welcomed and introduced to the congregation), in general in the movement, one's member status is reckoned as accruing by virtue of one's having completed one's course of study. On that basis one is admitted as part of the group.

New Membership classes help prepare new members for the type of learning experience they will encounter once they enter the main sanctuary and begin attending services regularly. "Knowing" certain things is one of the principle means of attaining insider status in the Word of Faith community.[5] The movement sees itself as possessing knowledge that is not taught in denominational churches. Thus their churches are referred to as "teaching" ministries, the people "know who they are in Christ," and they claim to have access to greater levels of blessing than others because of what they know and believe. So "knowing" holds an extremely important place in the movement, and this priority can be seen at work in the process by which new members are inducted into the congregation at Faith Christian Center.[6]

The Faith Message in the Worship Service: Teaching versus Preaching

Along with the emphasis on education and knowing who you are in Christ, there is also a corresponding emphasis on the job, or "calling," of teaching. A high priority is placed upon teaching congregants rather than merely preaching to them. In his book *Prosperity on God's Terms*, Frederick K. C. Price, one of the most prominent of today's Faith teachers, writes:

> One of my ministerial assignments from God is to teach His Word
> in simple, direct, layman's terms so that anyone from anywhere
> with an open heart and mind can hear, learn, and profit thereby. . . .
> Faith, healing, the Holy Spirit, and, of course, prosperity are areas in
> which the Lord has led me to concentrate my *teaching* ministry.[7]

Rather than a sermon, as in more traditional churches, in the Word of Faith Movement, the pastor or other speaker sees himself or herself as coming to instruct, to deliver information and insight—new "revelation," as it were—from God to the people. The purpose of this information and revelation is to equip and prepare believers to apply biblical principles in practical ways in the course of their daily lives. There is a conscious though selective disavowal of the sermonic traditions commonly associated with the Black Church and certain other forms of Protestant Christianity. This disavowal does not extend to all aspects of the sermonic tradition but primarily to that part of it that emphasizes and consciously seeks to achieve an emotionally charged, collective, emotionally cathartic experience. Aspects of this sermonic tradition can still be found in certain points and in certain ways throughout the worship services however. In contrast with the freedom of emotional and ecstatic display in many traditional African American religious groups, Word of Faith ministers seek to achieve a collective moment of intellectual clarity, leading to what they call a "quality decision" to do any or all of the following: to convert (or return to the faith for those who might have backslid), to accept the premise of the day's message as true and applicable, or to accept the invitation to join the church. In other parts of the Black sermonic tradition, congregants are still expected to respond to the minister's statements with loud "Amen"s of agreement; they are expected to clap and give other types of outward responses in the co-construction of the message with the minister.

In keeping with its New Thought roots, the Faith Message seeks to achieve the effective transformation of the way people *think*, a renewing of the mind, which will, in turn, bring about a transformation in the decisions individuals make on a daily basis. Believers are encouraged not to be conformed to the things of this world but to be transformed by the renewing of their minds. They are not encouraged to be transformed by some instantaneous, short-lived, emotionally based experience of the Holy Ghost in rapturous worship—but by a continual, long-term renewal of their thought patterns and their most basic daily decisions. This distinction is essential to understanding how the Word of Faith Movement differs from traditional Pentecostalism while still retaining some of its doctrinal positions. It is yet another example of the way in which this contemporary movement mixes codes, picking and choosing from among a variety of culturally available elements from various sources, recombining them into new and different patterns of belief and practice.

Delivery of the message is structured very much like a university lecture or a business seminar. Congregants are encouraged to come to church with pens, pencils, note tablets, and highlighters so as to be able to take notes and to mark certain passages of scripture as directed by the speaker. Some even come to church with briefcases in which they carry more than one translation of the Bible as well, along with other supplies. They have not come to church only to worship; they have come to *learn* as well. The speaker (almost invariably the pastor in Sunday services) often refers to having conducted research in preparation to bring the day's message to the congregation. In many respects, these services are much less like traditional Pentecostal services and much more like a presentation at a professional meeting or a colloquium. These biblical research presentations are offered on a weekly basis, not only on Sunday mornings but also in midweekly Bible studies and on any other occasion when a speaker will address the congregation with a specially prepared message.

At times, the congregation is instructed to read aloud from scripture, following along with the speaker. They keep themselves ready, their Bibles near, fingers poised. Sometimes congregation members playfully compete with the pastor or each other to be first to reach the scripture that is called out for them to turn to in their Bibles. This exercise subtly communicates, especially to newcomers, the value placed on being familiar with the order of books of the Bible as signifying that they are spending time studying it when they are not at church. The individual who quickly finds the scripture and shouts "Amen" or (some other phrase given them to shout when they reach it), is assumed to be more spiritual or disciplined outside of church than those who fumble or have to look at the table of contents. This is very subtle, but it is another way the values of the church are reinforced in the context of interaction in the services.

Individuals are encouraged to review the notes they take during the service in their personal Bible study time. Their Bibles are used as personal workbooks, as speakers will often instruct the congregation to underline or circle certain words. Many people also use colored highlighting pens in their Bibles to mark off certain passages. This practice not only differs from a more traditional use of the Bible as a sacred text but also is deemed a sacrilege or a desecration by some outside the movement. This use of the Bible is not exclusive to the Word of Faith Movement, but the emphasis on believers' being able to both name specific biblical promises and claim them for themselves, personally, leads to a way of approaching scripture that is much more instrumental than the meditative or introspective way many other evangelicals use the Bible. Believers are encouraged to "own" the Bible and its promises in a highly personalized way.

Teaching, learning, and knowing in the Word of Faith church service reflect what might be called the dialectical or research model. From the beginning to its end, the message takes the following form: a case is constructed, a claim made, and the scriptural evidence of the Bible is adduced as support and proof, leading to a decision to accept or refute the initial claim: thesis, antithesis, evidence, and finally synthesis. This is quite different from the ways sermons have traditionally been structured and carried out in the Holiness-Pentecostal church service according to many who have left them for Word churches. This use of the Bible as the source of evidence in the presentation of the message teaches people to verify what they are being taught (in church and by other ministers on television or radio, or by people in general) by doing their own research in the Bible.

Interestingly, within the Word of Faith Movement there are very few "hellfire-and-brimstone" messages about the need of repentance in order to avoid the pit of hell. The major emphasis in the message is on individuals learning how, through faith, to appropriate God's provisions and promises in the Bible for themselves and also how to be better, more prosperous, Christians in all areas of life.[8] During these times of instruction, vocal outbursts and ecstatic spontaneity (like the stylized type of dancing known as "shouting" in traditional Pentecostal churches) are discouraged. People do, however, still exclaim "Amen" and clap their hands in patterned response and punctuation to the speaker's words, as well as during certain high points in the message. This is all part of what has been carried over from the sermonic tradition, the "call-and-response" form of preaching and collective participation so characteristic of the religious traditions of many predominately African American churches.

That is not to say that there is no place at all for free, unfettered ecstatic expression in the worship services. Expressive worship is still there, but it exists within a structured sense of decorum that distinguishes it from Holiness-Pentecostal worship style. There are times in which some one of a small number of regulars—who are recognized by the pastor as legitimately possessing a certain spiritual gift and are thus allowed to address the assembly as such an instrument—will begin speaking aloud in tongues. This usually occurs at the end of the Praise and Worship congregational singing part of the service. When this happens, everyone else will be quiet and listen as the person goes forth in tongues. When they finish, someone is expected to bring the interpretation. Sometimes the person who spoke in tongues will also be the one to interpret. If no one starts "interpreting" within a reasonable passage of time, the pastor will declare that somebody has the interpretation and that they should "bring it forth." If no one speaks, he will sometimes do it himself, thereby adding to the sense that what the congregation had stopped to listen to was indeed a type of "instant message" directly from God. In this way, what might seem to be little more than a disorderly outburst to an outsider actually becomes part of the interactional order of the service. It is within the range of acceptable behaviors at the correct point in the proceedings.

In this church and in the context of the worship services led by him, the pastor determines when someone's manifestation of the Spirit (or any other type of "outburst") is *or is not* legitimate and whether it is to be acknowledged by the congregation as such. It is the pastor who legitimates these outbursts or quashes them if the interpretation given is deemed "off" or somewhat negative and therefore "not of God." It is he who defines the situation in terms of behavioral norms of what is or is not appropriate in the setting, and he has no problem publicly confronting or censuring someone in the midst of the congregation. Two examples serve to illustrate this point. The first occurred in a highly charged evening service at which a guest speaker was present. After Praise and Worship, a woman on the other side of the auditorium from where I was seated continued to stand and call out things like "Hallelujah, thank you, Jesus!" even after the music had stopped, everyone was seated, and one of the ministers was giving the welcome remarks. As she continued to shriek loudly, several of the ushers approached. Within minutes of beginning, she was lifted up by six male ushers (known as the "Royal Guards" here), held aloft, and bodily removed from the service in a matter of seconds. Order was restored.

On another occasion the pastor was in the midst of his Sunday morning message concerning the topic of grace when down in one of the front rows a woman, one of the members of the Overcomers' Program, jumped up and started shouting "Thank you, Jesus!" with arms outstretched. Some of the ushers and security staff began to approach her, but the pastor turned to them and said "She's okay, leave her alone. She's probably going through something right now." These two examples show that not all spontaneous, ecstatic outbursts are interpreted the same way by the pastor, who has the power to decide whose behavior is appropriate and whose behavior warrants being bodily removed from the service.[9] But the designated spaces in which expressive worship is given a hearing are subject to rather strict time constraints. This brings us to another example of the move away from complete freedom of expression in the course of the worship service: the way time is used.

Timeliness is a highly valued virtue in Word of Faith churches. Some of this attention to time might be a function of the incursion of television cameras into the setting. When being taped, speakers have to monitor the length of their address to fit within specific time constraints for broadcast media use. Television cameras, with brightly lit digital counters, tick off the seconds and minutes backward from the beginning of the message to its end. The pastor usually takes 45 minutes for delivering his message. At the end of his time, the headsetted camera operators can sometimes be seen giving him signals to wrap up the message. Those present in the service can clearly see these signals and can also see the seconds counting down on the cameras. Thus the camera is not an invisible presence; all are fully aware of its existence and work to shape their behavior accordingly.

The importance of the Christian knowing who he or she is in Christ is also the basis for all teachings on this-worldly prosperity that have come to characterize the movement (particularly among its detractors). If knowing who they are and what they deserve as Christians is the basis for prosperity, then providing an intellectual structure for them to learn and acquire this all-important information becomes vital. The pastor (or other teacher) becomes a facilitator of the individual's enlightenment, of learning who one is and what one can legally ask of God and expect to receive, based upon the Bible as God's Will and Testament, a binding agreement between the Creator and the Christian.

In order for believers to obtain and then to exercise the strong faith that is to lead to their prosperity, health, and general well-being, they must know certain things and not just feel them. Feelings are not to be trusted, due to their temporal and transitory nature. Only the Bible, the Word of God, is to be trusted as the final and literal arbiter of Truth.

The Faith Message and the Needs of the Ministry

The Doctrine of "Helps" and the Demand for Workers

Running a large ministry, especially one with so many departments, outreaches, and basic needs, requires a large volunteer labor base in addition to the relatively small staff of paid employees. It is frequently heard at Faith Christian Center that there are not enough available and willing people to do the ongoing work of the ministry, and appeals for members to come out and help are many. The organizational needs of the ministry are given sacred significance, as they are constructed in such a way as to shape and reshape some of the contours of the Faith Message being taught in the congregation. That is, the organizational needs of the church are articulated liturgically and presented to the people in the context of their expectation of prosperity and blessing from God.

Having completed the New Membership classes and now having all the rights and privileges accruing to any other member, it is then time for new members to "get busy" in the ministry, as they are so frequently reminded when they are fellowshipped in as new members. At this point one is also required to attend Ministry of Helps classes before starting to work in any part of the ministry—whether in the nursery, the choir, or as one of the all-male corps of ushers, the Royal Guards. The format for the "Helps" classes is similar to that of the New Membership classes: there is a specified number of required lessons and an attendance card that is used to verify that the person actually came to all of them. The primary focus in these classes is different, however. Students are taught that service to the church and the pastor is each member's personal ministry and has been mandated by God. It is God's will for every member to have a job working, volunteering in the church (according to scripture of course); it is not a matter of personal choice but of spiritual obligation.

Each week in these classes the students are directed to scriptures throughout the Old and the New Testaments offering examples of various figures serving and helping others in some capacity or another. In particular, attention is drawn to those instances in which his followers, those closest to him, are serving some "man of God" or other (as he serves them by seeking God on their behalf). Because of their help, the man of God is able to fulfill the work that he has been sent to do. A frequently cited Old Testament example is the story (in Exodus) in which Moses, as leader of the Israelites in their 40-year wilderness sojourn, is instructed by his father-in-law to divide the people and set men over them in order to administer the needs of the people. Other wellworn examples of biblical leadership and delegation of responsibility can be found throughout the New Testament and together they form the scriptural basis for church work.

Many people leave these classes excited and eager to get to work in some capacity or another. If there is a pressing need in a particular ministry, some new members may actually start working before finishing their Helps classes, but they are encouraged to complete them as soon as possible thereafter. Theoretically, one can be a member in the church without working in the ministry, but the pressure to do so comes very quickly after joining and doesn't usually subside until you capitulate and others actually see you working in the ministry. For example, a particular midweek Bible study featured a lesson on helping the man of God. At the conclusion of that evening's teaching, those not working in the ministry—regardless of the reason—were instructed by the pastor that on this particular issue they were all "in sin" and needed to immediately repent and ask God for his forgiveness.

These free riders were told that they should repent for the sin of standing by and allowing the pastor and those already working and burned out in the ministry to continue to do the lion's share of the work of running the ministry. They were reminded that the ultimate goal of the church and everyone who was a member was the saving of more souls. Given the large number of people that made up the ministry, he should never have to "beg" people to help run it. All those who did not have a ministry job were then asked to stand and repeat aloud a prayer, or public confession, of repentance led by the pastor. They were all then directed to immediately come up front into the choir stand to sign up for the Helps classes *and* to leave their contact information so they could be placed in an available ministry job as soon as possible.

This type of public self-disclosure—confession, contrition, and repentance—is common at Faith Christian Center and appears to be recurring more frequently in gatherings of the church body. The expectation that all members be active in the ministry exerts great demands on its members. Through public self-disclosure, those who do not conform to this expectation are publicly censured, and sanctions are brought to bear upon them and their behavior as members of this community.

Sowing Seeds of Prosperity: Money, the Local Church, and the Faith Message

As with any other human service organizations, running a church requires money. The physical expansion of Faith Christian Center and the increasingly large numbers of people it serves through its more than 120 programs (as well as in its worship services and various Bible studies) places an ever-increasing need for the continued, *generous* financial support of the congregation and others (like those who watch the television broadcasts). The pace of the ministry's expansion accelerated in the mid-1990s, as the new church structure neared completion following several years of a building program, named "Dreams Alive," that solicited special offerings and pledges from the congregation. The new building accommodated far more people than the previous structure. With more room, more people came to the ministry with more needs to be met.

The principle means by which this financial support is achieved is through the collection of offerings during the course of every worship service (three on Sunday alone, as well as other special services) and in the various Bible studies held throughout the week. The doctrine of the Faith Message emphasizes great, supernatural promises of financial prosperity for the believer, but that promise of prosperity is linked very closely to one's continued support of the financial needs of the local ministry through openhanded and consistent donation of money to one's local church. Tithing, the Old Testament practice of giving the church 10 percent of one's gross—not net—income from every source, is depicted as more than just giving money. It is seen as a rite of worship and devotion to God. According to this explanation, tithing is a sign of gratitude for God's having blessed the individual with this income in the first place, and giving the tithe expresses obedience to the biblical examples of the believers supporting the needs of the priests and the temple/organizational church as it later developed.

Tithing is not uncommon among Christian groups and is by no means exclusive to this movement. What is distinctive and noteworthy in the Faith Message is the fact that the practice of regular tithing and the giving of offerings over and above one's 10 percent are conceptualized not only as an act of devotion but as sowing or "planting seeds." It is according to the biblical "law," based upon the way God created the natural world to operate, that one who "sows" finances should expect to "reap" a harvest of financial blessing in return. It's the same as when one plants apple seeds: unless something goes wrong, you can and should expect to receive a harvest of apples. Accordingly, corn seeds yield a corn harvest, flower seeds yield flowers, and so on. Believers are always chided that they should never miss an opportunity to be blessed by giving money into offerings. These opportunities for giving include alms for the poor; missions offerings to support overseas missionaries; and "love" offerings that are presented as a gift to a visiting minister or performer. The congregation are taught that when they contribute their money to these offerings, they should expect to receive money as a return on their investment. They are not just giving money; they are planting financial seeds, making a spiritual investment.

The Faith Message is being shaped by the material needs of the ministry. The financial needs of the ministry have obviously increased: a larger building to cool in the summer and keep warm in winter, the addition of lights and cameras to tape services for broadcast, a more powerful sound system, and every other material aspect of the day-to-day operation of this physical plant. Thus the emphasis on giving money to the church and supporting it financially has also greatly increased. Parallel with the ministry's expansion into the new building, the frequency with which the sermons refer to and associate giving money with financial prosperity seems to have increased dramatically.

Language, regarding one's financial status, is very important. On the Sundays during which special alms offerings are taken up to help the poor, the pastor instructs the congregation: "We here at Faith don't take up alms for the 'poor,' we collect offerings for those who are 'between the blessings'—how many of *you* have ever been between the blessings?" A number of those in the congregation respond with raised hands and nods of agreement or by affirming their response with someone sitting nearby. This is another way in which the teaching about confession is expressed in this culture. To call someone *poor* here implies that poverty is a permanent or intrinsic characteristic of his or her being (or that it will engender that state in him or her by having spoken poverty as a curse "over" him or her). Redefining poverty as a state of being "between blessings," implies that poverty is only a temporary lack of money and not a long-term social location or identity that one should accept.

Second, asking the audience whether they had ever personally been "between blessings" encourages identification with the plight of the less fortunate. This serves as an encouragement to give into these special offerings (which are usually taken after the regular offerings have been collected). This powerful rhetorical device also invokes for givers a notion of their having overcome and progressed beyond that lower state themselves to the higher economic level they now occupy. Appealing to people to remember when they may have been in the same position reminds them how greatly they may have been blessed financially. In turn, this appreciation of how they have been blessed is supposed to lead to generosity in giving to those less fortunate in their midst. Those who are "between blessings" are not imagined as a group separate from the rest of the congregation—they are not The Poor outside the church walls—but are here in the midst of those giving alms. After all, everyone has been or is between some blessing or another.

The self-consciously creative use of words is a very common feature of the Word of Faith Movement as a subculture. On one occasion, I had the opportunity to informally interview a couple of first-time visitors immediately after the service they had attended. It was Multicultural Sunday, and they were young Anglo-Americans in their early twenties. When, over breakfast, I asked what they had thought of the service, their first—and most emphatic—reaction was to the "between the blessings" phrase. They said they had never quite heard being "broke" referred to in that way before. Their apparent delight and amusement at this church's use of words is not an uncommon reaction among those visiting the church for the first time or seeing a Faith teacher on television. Although they did not return for additional services, this particular young man and woman were sufficiently impressed with this reconceptualization of the state of financial lack that they continued to invoke and repeat it long afterward, whenever they were faced with "financial challenges" (another common term by which temporary shortages of money are redefined in the Word of Faith Movement).

Of all the particulars of doctrine taught at Faith Christian Center, tithing would have to be numbered among the most frequently and strongly emphasized. Tithing is not a practice distinctive to the Word of Faith Movement, but it is at the root of much of the teaching about giving money and to the expectation of financial blessings as a direct result. Certain scriptures (mostly from the Old Testament) are used to show that tithing *at least one-tenth of one's gross income* is an act of worship and is part of the commandment God has placed on the Christian—especially those who want to be *protected* from a curse of poverty and blessed with prosperity by God (especially in terms of material wealth).

For example, Malachi 3:6–12 is frequently used to teach that tithing is God's will for today's believer, and that great reward accompanies or follows obedience, while a curse accompanies or follows disobedience to this edict. This often-quoted passage reads:

> Will a man rob God? Yet ye have robbed me. But ye say, Wherein have we robbed thee? In tithes and offerings. Ye are cursed with a curse: for ye have robbed me, even this whole nation. Bring ye all the tithes into the storehouse, that there may be meat in mine house, and prove me now herewith, saith the Lord of hosts, if I will not open you the windows of heaven, and pour you out a blessing, that there shall not be room enough to receive it. And I will rebuke the devourer for your sakes, and he shall not destroy the fruits of your ground; neither shall your vine cast her fruit before the time in the field, saith the Lord of hosts. And all nations shall call you blessed: for ye shall be a delightsome land, saith the Lord of hosts.

This passage is frequently invoked and taught in Word of Faith Movement churches to instill a sense of fear alongside the expectation of great financial blessings available to those who will faithfully "pay" their tithes. Those who fail to pay are taught they (or, more accurately, their finances) are cursed, unprotected, exposed, and vulnerable to attack (by the Devil). They have willfully chosen not to trust God to meet their needs, instead paying a utility bill or the mortgage with God's money, defined as "stolen" money. As a result of members' bringing God's money into the storehouse, the church, the needs of the ministry are met without resort to such supposedly poverty-driven devices as selling chicken dinners or donating used clothing to finance God's kingdom. The pastor frequently and proudly proclaims that "not one chicken gave his life for this ministry" [the way Christ gave His life for the church], referring to the type of fundraising programs that many smaller, non–Word of Faith Movement, or denominational churches routinely conduct. These churches have to "resort" to these undignified programs because their pastors, presumably, are not teaching their members about the biblical curse and blessings promised by God to those who consistently tithe.

In recent years in the ministry, there has been a great deal of talk and teaching about what is referred to as "the corporate anointing." According to those in leadership positions, this corporate anointing represents the power of God to move on behalf of the entire body of believers as an entity. Once they have been given the official interpretation of it by the pastor or other teachers, those who do not consistently or "correctly" tithe are subsequently defined as a hindrance to the rest of the congregation. It is presumed, of course, that everyone else is faithfully and correctly tithing themselves. Those not tithing are told they are blocking the others from receiving their abundant blessings as reward for their faithfulness in giving money to God through the medium of the local church. Those not tithing (again, regardless of whether they think they are able to spare the money in light of other financial obligations) are then made responsible and culpable for the rest of the congregation's not being able to receive the prosperity they have been promised and are entitled to. Their supposed disobedience to the command of the 10 percent tithe is read back to them as signifying their lack of trust in God to meet their needs, including ensuring that the needed rent, utilities, and food are provided for them and their families.

It is also not uncommon in the course of services for the pastor or another minister to ask those not tithing—as is done in the case of those not working in the ministry, regardless of their individual reasons—to stand up in an act of public disclosure and repentance. Public shaming and the diffusion of responsibility for ensuring and not hindering the prosperity of everyone in the ministry are both at work in the practice. A sophisticated form of peer pressure is used to liturgically reinforce the need for members' continued financial support of the ministry.

Of course, people may choose not to publicly (or even privately) disclose such personal information, but a great many do stand and accept it, presumably, and at least partially, because of the fear that some sort of curse will befall them or that God will remove any protection or favor from them. In the previous chapter one respondent spoke about being afraid not to give lest some calamity befall her. Fran was one of those who expressed great ambivalence at the Faith Message's teachings on sowing financial, monetary seeds and expecting to receive a harvest of money in return for one's giving. Many of the ministers encourage this fear, continually invoking it when instructing members about their responsibility for financially supporting the ministry. Members are told that by not giving (or giving less than they should) they have effectively "opened themselves up" to any number of catastrophic situations by which they may lose even what money they now have. Of course, one could simply remain seated and no one would know one's personal financial-spiritual situation. But in this atmosphere, in which so much is believed to be promised to the believer from God, and the threatened consequences of not doing what the pastor says (because he is God's representative, after all) are so dire, standing up and suffering the embarrassment or public humiliation may seem better than incurring God's wrath by not giving at all. Standing up and publicly re-

penting also ushers these transgressors back into the fold after such an egre-
gious offense; reconciled back to the body of believers, and presumably returned to the will of God.

Thus, liturgically, the promise of great, supernatural levels of prosperity
(the opening of the windows of heaven) serves as a powerful carrot, while the
threat of the curse and of being a hindrance not only to one's own prosperity
but also that of one's neighbor provides an equally (if not, for some people,
more) powerful stick with respect to their giving behavior. Since the material
needs of the ministry have increased in the last few years, it appears that the
degree of emphasis on giving money, especially tithes, has also increased. Co-
incidentally, several visiting ministers have all brought the same "special" message to the congregation: that they all needed to be tithing and supporting the
ministry financially if they wanted to be greatly, supernaturally, "outrageously"
blessed in their finances as their reward from God. The people are taught that
the correlation between the two is direct and that it is causal.

At Faith Christian Center there are also many other opportunities to plant
financial seeds in addition to tithes: one may make several types of offerings,
and one may support the programs to build and pay for the new church structure and to purchase new properties, such as an abandoned nursing home that
the church wants to convert into a school. Members are told that they should
remain on the alert for these offerings and always be prepared to contribute.
Sometimes members are presented with specific requests, defined as "opportunities," to bless the pastor and/or his family and "sow into good ground."
Typically, a member of the church staff announces that a particular gift has
been chosen for a particular occasion, like a birthday or anniversary, and that
they want to present the gift on that day, as well as an accompanying cash gift.

It is not uncommon for the pastor and his wife to be presented with gifts
like matching Rolex watches or cars, including a Jeep Cherokee given by a
group of men in this ministry, and a BMW given to the pastor's wife by another
congregation (and later a Jaguar from another group of givers). For one of their
wedding anniversaries, the pastor and his wife were presented with a 10-day
cruise that included passage through the Panama Canal. During the planning
stages, before they were presented with the tickets, the congregation was told
that their donations would finance the trip and an accompanying cash gift. At
another time, the Pastor's Appreciation Day program included a special presentation of more than one cash gift, again reportedly from the congregation's
offerings as well as from some famous Word of Faith Movement donors like
Fred and Betty Price (of Crenshaw Christian Center) and Kenneth and Gloria
Copeland (of Kenneth Copeland Ministries). The list of donors was read in the
midst of the service devoted to showing appreciation and love for the pastor,

the "gift from God" to the ministry. On that day people also continued to give monetary gifts directly to him throughout the service. In April 1999 the pastor turned 50 years old. Six months beforehand, the church administrator announced to the congregation that the staff and planning committee wanted to give the pastor a formal dinner as his birthday party and that the cost of the tickets would be $300 per couple. The price included the dinner and the gift that would be given him. Those in the audience that day were told that if the price seemed too high, they could start saving for it immediately by putting away a little each month for the next six months.

None of the ways in which financial gifts have been given to the pastor and his family is unique to this church or to the Word of Faith Movement. But in this context they demonstrate some of the ways in which giving is redefined in terms of the Faith Message and its doctrine of sowing seeds of financial prosperity, expecting great financial return. These instances of giving are defined for the congregation as opportunities for sowing seed into good ground, ground that would produce a "hundredfold return." But in the context of a multitude of programs that are financed primarily through the monetary contributions of the congregation, made up of many working-class people who are themselves "between blessings," these lavish gifts are requested with all seriousness and with the expectation that people who wanted to participate would actually begin saving $25 or $50 per month for six months in order to finance a fiftieth birthday party for their pastor.

To those who think the Word of Faith Movement is on theologically shaky ground, what seems troubling is the *attitude*, which they see as arrogant and presumptuous, reflected in movement members' "placing a demand on God" and expecting him to fulfill what they see as his promises of prosperity, based on their reading of the Bible. Leaders seem not to have a problem with asking for what appear to be outrageously extravagant gifts from the members because they do believe that God has the will to honor those gifts in kind. A frequently invoked scriptural passage is Luke 6:38, which reads: "Give and it shall be given unto you, good measure, pressed down, and shaken together, and running over, shall men give into your bosom. For with the same measure that you mete withal, it shall be measured to you again."

The financial demands placed on the people in the ministry are great. But the "larger-than-life," lavish, extravagant financial blessings held out as God's plan for them renders completely rational the idea of sowing seeds into good ground like the pastor and his family because members are taught they will indeed reap a harvest on their giving. As they have sown finances, so shall they also reap finances, and the windows of heaven shall be opened unto them.

Dealing with Diversity: The Faith Message and Building the "Rainbow" Church

Each month as part of the Multicultural Sunday program the pastor instructs the people that he has been given a mandate from God that Faith Christian Center is to become one of the largest (if not the largest) multicultural (and/or multiracial) congregations in the country. He then goes on to instruct the people that the Christian church, especially the denominational traditions, has allowed the walls of prejudice, ignorance, and bigotry to remain standing and separating Christians for far too long. Moreover, he says that the Word of Faith Movement is at the forefront of tearing those walls down by *teaching* people what the Bible *really* says about interracial interaction and reconciliation. The establishment of a truly multicultural church, however vaguely defined, becomes yet another part of a spiritualized commandment that is presented to the congregation liturgically. It then becomes incorporated into the doctrine in such a way as to position the Faith Message as the message directly from above, a new revelation, in this great movement of God for racial reconciliation in the contemporary Christian church.

The empirical reality of multiculturalism in the surrounding community is in itself quite compelling, even without a commandment directly from God. For example, following the collapse of the former Soviet Union, many Russian evangelicals, like Katia and her family, came to the United States, seeking freedom from persecution, and settled in the Sacramento area. Faith Christian Center is one of the churches in the area that has decided to reach out to this new immigrant population.

Although the pastor and the majority of the congregation (approximately 60–70 percent) are African Americans, the pastor is adamant that this is *not* a Black church but a "Rainbow," or "Bouquet," church. Data on the racial composition of the congregation are not collected, but it is clear to even the casual observer that the congregation is, indeed, diverse in racial and ethnic makeup. But it is also readily apparent that African American culture and worship style are still dominant in this setting—especially those Black Church traditions that many members have brought with them from the denominational churches. Examples include the dominant musical style of gospel in the services, the use of call and response during the message, and frequent references to Black denominational practices from "the first church" (like shouting, dancing, running around the church at high points in the service, and so on). Nevertheless, people of other racial and ethnic backgrounds can be seen in positions of authority and leadership on the ministerial staff, as language interpreters, and as part of the various ministries by which the church is run and renders service to the congregation and the surrounding community.

To avoid exclusionary and narrowly defined denominational, racial, and ethnic identifications (other than the frequently heard declaration "we are a rainbow here at Faith"), the church is named a "Christian Center," as against a possible Church of God in Christ or other denominational marker or identifier. The pastor has said that when he founded the church and prayed about what it should be called, he did not want people to come with preconceived ideas about the church's teachings, practices, based upon expectations drawn from denominational markers. The name "Christian Center" was a deliberate move to disaffiliate the church's nondenominational identity from the naming traditions of denominational Pentecostal organizations like the Church of God in Christ, which was founded by and has been populated primarily by African American Pentecostals since early in the twentieth century. By using a denominational marker like Church of God in Christ, the more traditionally oriented church organization proclaims and reaffirms its organizational and doctrinal position and affiliation. The name Christian Center is used to attract those looking for a sense of freedom from the dictates of what they see as doctrinal "denominationalisms" or for those people who associate certain denominational names with certain races or classes of people and might not come if they were put off by a denominational name denoting a Black church.

Also observable is the absence of traditional iconography in the decor of the church. There are no anthropomorphic representations of any kind. There is none of the portraiture, stained glass, or iconic statuary that might be found in more traditional churches or other types of religious organizations. What religious imagery there is generally incorporates the dove, the biblical symbol of the Holy Spirit, based upon the New Testament detail of Christ's baptism by John the Baptist. The dove is part of Faith Christian Center's corporate logo, which can be seen on official literature and products coming from the ministry. The complete lack of anthropomorphic images of the deity, saints, or angels avoids any vision or conception of God in the image of any particular racial or ethnic group. The leadership at Faith Christian Center is very much aware of, and speak frequently about the importance of, making people from all racial backgrounds feel included.

Another example of the way Faith goes about defining itself as inclusive can be seen in the use of interpreters in the services. At the beginning of most worship services, after one of the ministers gives the welcome message, he (usually a male) then hands the microphone over to an interpreter, who translates what was said into Spanish, and then another interpreter translates the welcome into Russian (at least one person also translates into sign language).

The words in both languages are projected on the two large monitors on either side of the platform in "real time," while the translations are being heard by all, so those who speak only those languages can also *read* their welcome. The church also provides non-English-speakers with a small headset through which they can hear a real-time translation of the entire service, including the songs, the dramatic skits, and the message. These are available to Spanish and Russian speakers. Special worship services have recently been added in which Spanish- and Russian-speaking congregants can worship together in their own language while still being part of the overall congregation.

The monthly Multicultural Sunday program is another way the church goes about constructing the rainbow church that is part of the pastor's God-given vision for the ministry. This program is not just about presenting a nice show for the people to enjoy. Multicultural Sunday is very much an expression of the demand for Christians to move past their own neighborhoods and to make primary-group connections with people outside their own racial groups. In order for the vision of a racially diverse ministry to be realized, members of Faith are strongly encouraged to engage in this form of outreach by being asked to stand with the person or persons from another race whom they have invited to church on each Multicultural Sunday. Those who have not brought such a guest are reminded that this is something they should be doing as part of their duty not only as Christians but also, more important, as members of this church, which has been given a mandate by God through their pastor.

In constructing the rainbow church, and in order to be a part of the Faith Christian Center ministry, one must realize that the scriptural pronouncement "To whom much is given, much is also required" applies directly and immediately to each and every member of the congregation. The meaning of the Faith Message held by the pastor and other ministers in the church and presented to the lay people is shaped by the *needs* of running such a large church with so many types of outreach to the surrounding community. The increased need for more volunteer workers and financial support of the ministry since the new, bigger building was completed is expressed in the increasing emphasis on the teachings about the giving of money and sowing seeds of financial prosperity. The need of the ministry to mentor new converts and address the growing immigrant population is expressed in the monthly Discipleship Sunday and Multicultural Sunday programs. It is also expressed in the way the Faith Message is held up as a doctrine that is on the vanguard of racial reconciliation—even though this has been a major discourse among contemporary Christians from a variety of denominational and independent groups—since the early 1990s while these non–Word of Faith Movement groups are depicted as either not doing enough or as implicitly sanctioning racial separatism.

The Faith Message informs the attitudes, behaviors, organizational structures, and ritual practices at Faith Christian Center in many ways. New members are socialized and welcomed into the local congregation, as well as the distinctive worldview of the movement at large, through a series of New Membership and Ministry of Helps classes. The doctrine informs the disavowal of the preaching and the sermonic traditions that are practiced in some non-Word churches in favor of an emphasis on the Word of Faith Movement churches being "teaching" ministries. This privileging of preaching over teaching further supports the self-image within the movement that members of Word churches have progressed beyond denominational (or other non–Word of Faith Movement) churches. Members are taught to see themselves as having progressed beyond the members of denominational churches in their levels of understanding and revelation of God's will as contained in the Bible. They see themselves as being blessed with financial prosperity and vibrant health because they are the ones who have been spiritually attuned and bold enough to claim God's promised prosperity as their own.

4

Negotiating the Demands of Membership at Faith Christian Center

God is not unrighteous to forget your work and labor of love,
Which ye have shewed toward his name, In that ye have ministered
to the saints, and do minister.

—Hebrews 6:10

For many people one of the greatest challenges as believers *and* as
members of large churches like Faith Christian Center is reconciling
the demands of their everyday lives and the frequently conflicting
ones that flow from being workers in the church. When the demands of life conflict with those of the church, many receive less
sympathy than they would have expected, especially when they feel
they are trying to "live out" the success and victory elements taught
and emphasized so greatly in the Faith Message. A young man,
Joshua, told me the following story. When he was an undergraduate
at a local community college, he once failed to show up for the Tuesday night Bible study where he was supposed to lead the Praise and
Worship service in place of the minister ("Minister Taylor") who
normally did it. Taylor had said that Joshua was being "groomed" to
take over the position, and he was being allowed to lead the congregational singing during a few of the midweek Bible studies and at
the Sunday night service, which was less formal than the Sunday
morning services. On this particular Tuesday evening, however,
Joshua needed to study for a final exam that was scheduled for the
following morning. As he had been told to do in a situation like

this, early Tuesday morning Joshua called the church to let Minister Taylor know he would not be there that evening and why. Since, according to Taylor's secretary, Taylor was not available, he left a message with her describing the situation and that night stayed home to study instead of going to Bible study.

When they met a few days later, Minister Taylor approached Joshua excitedly, and angrily demanded to know why he had not shown up to lead Praise and Worship for Bible study *and* why he had not afforded him the courtesy of calling to let him know. He leveled one of the most serious of charges directed at member/workers in this ministry: he said that Joshua was "not faithful." Joshua was crushed. As it turned out, Minister Taylor had somehow not gotten the phone message and had decided to go home early, rather than staying to attend the Bible study and to critique Joshua's performance after singing with him, as he had usually done. Due to this misunderstanding and lack of communication, neither of the men had been present to lead the songs (only the women, who were also part of the Praise Team), and Taylor had been "called on the carpet" by the pastor, who had also demanded an answer to why *he* hadn't been there (since it was *Taylor's* job, not Joshua's, after all).

In response to Taylor's tirade, Joshua tried to explain that he had had to study that night for a final exam the following day and that he had indeed called on Tuesday morning to inform Minister Taylor that he would not be there as his backup that night. Either the secretary had not given him the message, or he had simply overlooked it. Taylor replied that he didn't care about Joshua's final exam—that it didn't matter to him what else he was doing—the most important thing was for Joshua to be there to work when he was supposed to be there and to be "faithful." Joshua left the encounter frustrated, embarrassed, and confused. He was confused about how he was supposed to meet the demands of being a member and worker in the church while applying the teachings of the Faith Message that encouraged him to prosper in all pursuits, both secular and spiritual.

Joshua's story might be in some respects unusual; Minister Taylor's reaction was extreme. But this kind of situation is common at Faith Christian Center. Of course, Minister Taylor's reaction was shaped by the position he had been put in. But it illustrates a larger point: there is a deep contradiction, and some people find themselves in difficult positions as they attempt both to live out the teachings of the Faith Message and to serve the needs of the ministry.

Coping with the Demands of Being a Church Member

Four strategies emerged from my interviews with members, observations of their behavior, and my own experience as a member of Faith Christian Center. I have termed these strategies: *filtering, venting networks, break taking,"* and, finally, leaving altogether, or *leave taking.*

"You don't eat everything set before you on the table": Filtering

Filtering is the active, intentional practice of accepting certain parts of the pastor's interpretation of scripture (or definition of the situation in terms of practice) while consciously rejecting others. Awareness of this strategy is important to our understanding of the nuanced character of religious practice and serves as a corrective to a popular caricature of religious people uncritically accepting whatever they are taught by their leaders. Some, if not all, hearers actively and consciously pick and choose those teachings they deem applicable to their personal situations while ignoring or tuning out those parts they find irrelevant. While this is certainly nothing new in religious life, it is especially striking in contexts like the one at Faith Christian Center, in which ministers declare that their directives come directly from God himself. Picking and choosing among various points in religious doctrines in such a context is fraught with tension and complexity.

The pastor at Faith Christian Center (like other Word of Faith Movement teachers) presents his version of the Faith Message in a way (using such expressions as "the *uncompromised* Word of God") that implies that those who hear it should accept whatever revelation or interpretation he offers as authoritative and that his interpretation has not been shaped by extratextual concerns or the prevailing mood of the times. This expectation of unquestioned and uncritical reception and application is *implied by* and usually accompanied with a chain of scriptural references as evidence that what he is teaching really *is* the correct reading of the Word and will of God. This implication is also bolstered by the repeated challenges for members to "check out in the Word" for themselves, whatever the teaching is, to see that the pastor's interpretation is supported by scripture. In everyday conversation many church members routinely cite the pastor and his particular interpretation of certain doctrinal points, and there is abundant reinforcement for the authority of his reading of scripture and little room left for public dissent. The pressure to conform to the pastor's reading of scripture is pervasive and strong for members of the church.

But there are people within the congregation who *do* dissent and disagree with what is being taught on various issues, doctrinally, organizationally, and even politically. And while there is obviously some degree of consensus around certain basic doctrinal issues—otherwise, those members would surely not be in this particular type of church in the first place, let alone remain—there is dissension that is exercised subjectively as people hear the message being taught.

In the congregation are people with varying degrees of experience with religious instruction and church participation. Those who have never been members of a church body for any sustained period of time may have little or nothing with which to compare the teachings they hear. But over time and with more experience with doctrine (whether the Faith Message or another type of teaching) they have an opportunity to become more informed consumers. The practice of filtering seemed to be much more central a part of the spiritual and religious toolkit of some than of others. They seemed to have come to a point in their understanding and practice of the Faith Message where they felt comfortable adopting only those things they thought appropriate to their situation and experience and rejecting those they deemed less relevant.

Some respondents, on the other hand, spoke in ways that were very much in keeping with the pastor's, or the official, line of doctrine at Faith Christian Center. Russell, who had converted from the Judaism of his childhood to evangelical Christianity as an adult, and who was now a dedicated member of Faith Christian Center, brought insight to this issue. Asked whether there were ever any points of doctrine he personally disagreed with, his response was instructive indeed:

> I haven't. I know that Pastor is given more revelation in some areas—maybe in the teaching in the nineties that was different from his teaching in the eighties because he got a different revelation on what the teaching of the Bible was. I haven't found anything he taught that I thought was totally inaccurate. He might not have had his full revelation of it. I've heard teachings from other ministers that are inaccurate that I won't listen to. So, someone tells me that being baptized in the Holy Spirit and speaking in tongues is not of God, I've got to say "oh, well, turn them off." I've got it, and it works! When I hear someone say it's not God's will for me to prosper, then I have to say that that's not accurate and I don't listen to it. You learn to discern.

> When you hear something that, that doesn't flow with what you know the Bible teaches, don't just keep listening to it, and don't argue about it. You just turn them off and pray.

When Russell says that he does not argue with someone who has a different understanding of the Bible and does not continue to listen to them but just turns them off and prays, he is articulating a teaching of the church he attends as well as one that is commonly heard from leaders in the Word of Faith Movement at large. Many in the movement believe they have been given the new revelation of God's mind and will for the church and the world. If anyone disagrees with them, then it is the dissident who is in error. Russell's assertion that you learn to discern could probably be heard from a member of many other evangelical religious bodies. However, it illustrates the position that the Word of Faith Movement teaches its members to take in the face of challenges from outsiders: do not engage in argument or debate, and do not allow validity to any of their criticisms. A significant part of what you "know" the Bible teaches is shaped by the present state of revelation from God through the pastor to the congregation. What you "know" the Bible teaches, then, might be subject to change as the pastor's revelation develops and changes over time.

I asked Russell if he could remember any topic or specific doctrinal point on which the pastor may have had an incomplete revelation and later came back with a different interpretation or emphasis in his subsequent teaching:

> Sure. I think that for a long time we were taught on this "binding and loosening" [sic], according to Matthew 18:19. For a long time, I was binding the wrong thing and loosing the wrong thing. And now I've got revelation that we *bind* what is good *to us* and *loose* what is bad *from us*.
>
> Versus what was the *old way*—binding what was bad and loosing what was good. We're loosing money. Loosing ministering angels to go get money. Well, you don't *loose* an angel to go get something for you. You *send* an angel to go get something. You loose a hindering spirit from that. You don't bind the spirit to somebody, because when you bind a spirit to somebody, then that attaches to them and you don't want that attached to them. Unless you're praying a *positive* spirit. Binding the spirit of love to someone. Binding the spirit of thanksgiving to someone. Binding the Word of God to someone. Binding the will of God to someone. But I don't—I'm not going to any longer, bind an evil spirit. I'm going to *loose* an evil spirit.

This is an example of a situation in which the pastor has taught some point of doctrine or practice and later comes back and revises the teaching, based on new revelation. His admission that he had been "binding the wrong thing and loosing the wrong thing" was in reference to a lesson that the pastor has previously taught the congregation and had just recently reversed. When asked if the pastor's coming later and saying that he has gotten a fuller revelation of some point or another (not that he has made a mistake) makes him begin to doubt, or question, his teachings or authority, Russell responded:

> No. No. Because I know more about some things than I knew before. I know more about automobiles than I did when I first started driving them. And if I go back and I do some more study, then I'm going to get some more insight. And there's a time when I might have been inaccurate. And if that's the case then I've got to say "Well, I've made a mistake," admit to it, and move on.

In this example, Russell says that he himself must admit to making a mistake or teaching something that is inaccurate. It appears from his comments, however, that he does not expect the pastor to have to do the same. The pastor of Faith Christian Center rarely says he has made a mistake in his previous teaching; rather, the way of constructing this according to charismatic values and the belief in continued and evolving revelation of God's eternal truths would be to frame it as receiving new revelation of doctrine ("hot off the press," as he frequently describes it). Russell went on to say:

> There have been some ministers in the past that have received offerings and it wasn't accurate what they were doing with the money. When I gave money into those ministries I was giving them in faith and as long as I was giving them in faith and I wasn't knowledgeable about things not being accurate then, then I believe the millions of people who are born again through ministries that preachers they may not be head of the ministries, but once the knowledge came then I said, "Okay, I don't support that any longer." But that doesn't mean there wasn't any fruit coming out of that. And I don't judge the entire ministry because it was a mistake that the individual made. And I don't need to be specific. That's not important. But if I find that's something not profitable, then you don't continue to support it.

To some observers, Russell's comments might suggest an uncritical stance toward what he hears and receives from his pastor. As mentioned in an earlier chapter, Russell has a strong sense of identification with his pastor. Remember that he has a photograph of the pastor and his wife in the entry-hall of his house, he related to me his age (49 at the time), saying it was "just like Pastor," and in a number of ways he indicated his loyalty to the ministry as well as to the man. He said that he does not experience any sense of doubt as a result of the pastor teaching one form of doctrine, based upon his present level of understanding and later coming back and teaching that same thing in a completely opposite manner—both times taught just as uncompromisingly.

To have a certain understanding of what scripture is saying means to have a certain way of *doing* something; to have an opposite (or simply different) understanding necessitates a change in the way the members do what they do as faithful Christians and members of the ministry. One case in point was the teaching concerning "binding and loosing" that Russell mentioned (and which was the current topic of the pastor's message series during this writing).

For years the pastor had taught that the scripture (Matthew 18:18) which reads: "Whatsoever ye shall bind in heaven shall be bound in earth, and whatsoever ye shall loose on earth shall be loosed in heaven." The prevailing interpretation as taught by the pastor was used by the members to shape their prayers and confessions. Members might be heard saying something like "I [or we] bind that spirit of anger, (or lust, or poverty, and so on) from operating in" [whomever is the subject/object of the prayer], "and I loose the ministering angels to watch over them and protect them." Recently, the pastor brought to the congregation a Sunday morning message in which he instructed the congregation that based upon his new revelation of binding and "loosening" (*sic*), they had been doing it wrong, and it was no wonder some of their prayers had not been answered. He then taught that according to his new revelation, one that he related that he had received, formulated, struggled, and prayed over for the past two years, they were to bind good things—the angels in the example— to them and loose bad things from them—like a bad spirit or the Devil. So the teaching was completely turned about from what it had been. Accordingly, how the people understood and used the concept or "spiritual principle" was replaced with a teaching that was completely reversed.

This was not an isolated incident. For example, when the pastor and his ministers—as part of the official doctrine of the church—taught the congregation that no matter what other financial obligation they had, they were to "pay their tithes" (from their gross income) first. According to the Faith Message's position concerning the link between God's promised prosperity and giving, they were to continually plant seed, unquestioningly obeying God (through the pastor's lips) while expecting him to provide *supernaturally* for their needs. Of course, many Bible stories were used in support of this belief. If there was any money left over afterward, then they could think about meeting their outstanding financial obligations like rent, utilities, gas for their cars, credit card bills, or food for their children. For many years this was the law of the land without compromise or exception, and those who were unable (or unwilling) to live a lifestyle of complete trust in God concerning their financial situation were labeled as rebellious, disobedient, or as lacking in faith.

However, years later the pastor said that he had received a different, new revelation concerning tithing: that it was God's plan for everyone to tithe from the gross of their income, but if they were not in a position to do this because of debt, or lack of money, and so on, then they were to repent to God that they'd not been a good steward (caretaker) of their finances and pray that they would some day be in a position to give 10 percent of their gross income. They were still instructed that they should give as much as they could (toward tithes, offerings, special projects like the building fund, school, etc.) but should actively seek to be out of debt so they could pay their tithes *and* their bills. Thus it was their skill at money management and the financial situation that needed to be changed in order to allow people to be *free* to obey God's commands now; earlier it had been a harsher position, in which people had to just trust God for their finances, even if that meant not paying a debt and choosing to pay tithes and apply one's faith that God would provide for one's household.

Lawrence, a 37-year-old married father of two, has worked in the ministry for many years as a musician. His comments offer further examples of the process of filtering. He explains why he can belong to a church in which he does not take in everything that proceeds from the mouth of the pastor, even though the pastor presents himself to the congregation as God's mouthpiece or messenger. Asked what allows him to remain part of a congregation and be in disagreement with some of the particulars of the teaching, he replied:

> If I understand your question correctly, it's my knowing that I have to be, for lack of better words, *skeptical* about what I'm taught. And in knowing that my common sense tells me I don't have to believe them. It can be filtering. And that is, "Okay, I can't accept this." Through the whole message I stayed. This is food, but for me this [part] is liver, and I don't eat [liver].

Lawrence clearly articulated that he thought it was actually his job to filter the doctrine coming down from the pastor or any other teacher, rather than accept it wholesale. He acknowledged that the pastor may indeed expect the congregation to receive his interpretation of scripture and of doctrine based on it without question, as truth through his lips from God. He continued:

> I strongly get that impression from [the pastor]. If I were in his position I would feel the same way. "This is the food that I have to feed

y'all. Y'all need to eat." Such as a mother tells a child. When that child gets older—especially when he starts to read and understand what food is good for him and comes to some understanding by life's experiences—he's going to say "Mom, hot dogs and corn flakes don't go together. I'm just going to eat something else and I'm going to leave this part of it out."

Lawrence offered a very specific example of the way he personally works out his understanding and use of the teachings and how these may differ from the way the teaching comes down from the pastor. Interestingly enough, that example involved the practice of tithing. We had been discussing his views on the prevalent teaching about seedtime and harvest, and Lawrence connected this concept to the point being emphasized in the messages that in order to receive financial blessings from God, one must continually plant financial seed in the form of money—especially the form of tithes and offerings—so frequently invoked in the services and in all the movement's teachings concerning money. He spoke of these two related issues as follows.

Okay, seedtime and harvest I honestly do believe. The way the Bible explains seedtime and harvest I honestly don't see how it could be false. Everything from actually giving money to bettering yourself in education so that you can have more seed and more harvest. There's nothing in the world that I know of that if you don't put more into it you get more out of it. There's nothing. You put gas in your car you get more mileage out. So, to me that's true. As far as tithes, I feel guilty when I can't. And maybe it's because I've been taught tithes from a younger age than what some other people have been taught. I do feel if I don't give anything then something's wrong. And there are those days when you just don't have enough to give. And you talk yourself into that 10 percent. You manipulate that thing to make it work for you if you have to. If your bills . . . if you get 1,000 dollars a month and your bills are 600 dollars and there's 400 dollars left, then tithes is 40 dollars. It's not the full 100 dollars. Because it ain't my money. It's someone else's.

So, contrary to what the pastor might be teaching concerning the proper way to tithe and the negative effects of not doing so, for Lawrence the desire to give and to tithe are more important than the exact numerical donation. Implied in the teaching is the message that if people do not give or do things a certain way, their offerings to God will not be acceptable to him. Numerous times in the services actions such as Lawrence's decision to tithe 10 percent of the money he had left over after bills would have been ridiculed from the pulpit as giving God a "tip," to great laughter (some of which might very well be guilty or nervous laughter) among members of the congregation.

Because the Faith Message is so strongly tied to directing people's everyday behavior in very practical, mundane matters like the management of their money, when faced with spontaneous, "new" revelations people must either accept all that the pastor teaches and then adjust their behaviors to stay in line with the changes in doctrine or actively filter what is being taught to tailor it to their own experience. The first of these two options can lead to a Christian life in which one's behavior might seem (especially to outsiders or critics) unstable. This state of apparent instability is the result of the fact that the pastor's teaching comes from his personal revelations and understandings of the Bible. The second option leaves one open to the charge of being "rebellious" when one's individual understanding is at odds with what is being taught. Members might feel that they are in engaged in a struggle that they can never win: to blindly follow their leader or to seek to implement their own understandings of scripture and lean on God's mercy if they should happen to be wrong. For some this issue is a major source of frustration within their Christian walk.

"You can't talk about these things with just anybody": Venting Networks

The second of the four strategies members use to negotiate the demands placed upon them at Faith Christian Center is the formation and use of what may be called *venting networks*. They emerge out of social interactions in which members—who may or may not be deemed "disgruntled" but who have something to say that may be interpreted by others as against the dominant view—are able to critique and to give voice to their disagreements or discontents concerning some aspect of their experiences in the church. In these networks they also have the freedom to express an understanding or interpretation of some part of the Bible that is at variance with the official reading as taught by the pastor and reinforced in interactions among many of the members.

Venting networks act as exhaust valves in an environment in which the pastor is practically absolute boss and the rank-and-file members sometimes appear distrustful of each other. There is sometimes a fear that if they express how they *really* feel about something, they risk being sanctioned, being labeled as "rebellious." They are taught to emulate the silent obedience of sheep. Scriptural examples of the evils and punishments that befall those who murmur and grumble, rather than simply following their God-appointed leaders, are often invoked. One of the commonly cited stories involves Moses leading the Israelites through the desert wilderness after their exodus from Egypt. The people continually complained about everything, even questioning Moses' leadership, and incurred God's wrath as a result. Sometimes the notion that they are to follow prayerfully but unquestioningly is the topic of the day's message, and these scriptural references are taught as examples of how *not* to behave. "Mute" obedience and submission to God's will, as expressed through the mouth of the pastor, is one of the highest values in this church. To openly question doctrine or the decisions of church leadership is interpreted as a challenge to the authority the people are encouraged to accept as God-given.

Venting networks exist on a continuum from spontaneous and situational to more long-term and stable. They can develop out of ordinary interaction and conversation, and they are not unlike those found in other settings. Such networks can be found in the workplace or among college students for example. But their development within a church is interesting. Just as in a secular setting, when there is not sufficient organizational space for adults to voice dissent or to simply question in order to gain more clarity on the actions of the group or organization, they need someplace to assert their own personhoods and to express their disagreements with other, like-minded adults. Members are being asked to donate their time, skills, labor, and, most of all, their money, when there are many other things competing for these resources. But many feel they are prohibited from questioning any point of doctrine or even church practice. When they try, the pastor or other members often tell them not to ask or challenge pastoral authority, which is God-given. They are told they should just pray if they think something is wrong with the way things are being done and believe that God will correct the leader if he happens to be indeed wrong. In this context, the potential for the emergence of venting networks is great, although the members are taught it is a sin to speak against the leadership of the church.

There are various ways that venting networks emerge. For example, two people might try to determine whether they can trust each other with their disclosure of their true feelings. For example, since members are expected to show up (either as an audience or as workers) at so many church-related activities held on a regular basis, one good way to find out if you can talk to someone is by asking them if they are planning to go (or if they went) to a particular event. From this opening, the way the person responds either furthers the discussion in the direction of a venting interaction or shuts it down from progressing further in that direction. With so many things happening in the church that people are expected to participate in, the way someone responds to this type of mundane query can communicate much about his or her feelings about the ministry (or that particular event).

I witnessed an encounter between two members of the ministry in which one asked the other if they were planning to attend the pastor's upcoming fiftieth birthday party and dinner. It was to be a formal affair, held at one of the local hotels, and it would cost over $100 per ticket. The response was an emphatic "No!" In this church that type of response would raise eyebrows. It would generally be interpreted to mean that the individual was not interested in celebrating the pastor's birthday (that he or she carried some sort of animosity toward him personally) or that he or she could not afford to attend because of not having the money. Seeming to feel as though she needed to clarify her position, the member offered a *third* reason why she was not planning to go. This involved disagreement with what she saw as the church's recent overemphasis on financial prosperity, the ostentatious displays of consumption, and the financial strain that this sort of thing placed on less wealthy members. This provided an opening to a discussion in which both members were able to vent—to get some things off their chests. But these two members had known each other for many years, and a certain level of trust had already been established prior to this particular instance of interaction.

Over the years, I have witnessed (or participated in) innumerable instances of this kind of coded exchange with other members who, it usually has turned out, have had something to vent and no one else to do it with. If the person asking the question had appeared offended or taken aback at the respondent's emphatic no (or if he or she seemed to be defensive or to be admonishing) the conversation would probably not have continued in the direction that it did. The second member might not have felt free to voice her philosophical objections to a birthday party that cost over $100 per person to attend. Thus venting networks are situated and contextual.

Another way these networks are established is when people say (when they perceive someone's hesitance to speak of a problem or situation) "Don't worry, you can be real with me," or "You don't have to use positive confession with me, you can speak freely." Depending on the level of trust that exists between them, the conversation will continue in this vein or be moved away from the topic concerning which the person may have a dissenting, or negative, opinion, or comment. This is an example of the way the principle of positive confession constrains the boundaries of members' acceptable speech even with each other. Even to voice a problem or negative situation in some way or another gives it power and an existence it wouldn't have if one didn't speak of it at all.

"Every good soldier deserves a break from battle":
Break Taking as Negotiation

The third strategy members use to cope with the demands placed upon them is that of taking breaks. I define break taking as voluntarily removing oneself either from one's position in the church as a worker for a period of time before returning at some later date or staying away from the ministry altogether for a period of time. In either case, people who take a break usually plan to return to the church and eventually do so. I found this to be one of the ways those who work in the ministry, and even some who don't, can establish some level of autonomy and a sense of identity and self-assertion and control over their lives and time. It is a way to live a life as a church member that is not completely dominated by one's role as a worker in whichever ministry department one happens to function.

Break taking is also used as a way of getting away from the familiar environment of the their home church and their routine in it. In fact, for some people, this seems like their only alternative: to actually leave the ministry for a while—a few weeks, months, or even years. Some of my interviewees spoke of being away from the church for two to three years before coming back and reestablishing themselves as working members. In the meantime, they may be visiting other churches, doing non-church-related activities, or just sleeping in on Sunday mornings. Commonly, when a worker wishes to take a break from performing a ministry job and just come to church as a regular member—this is known as "sitting down under the Word"—they are confronted by their colaborers or other people who are simply accustomed to seeing them up and about, doing certain duties and fulfilling certain functions in the service.

In addition to the peer pressure placed on those who may be physically and emotionally tired and just want to come to church to receive some sense of spiritual renewal, the pastor may also confront someone who is sitting down and ask why he or she is not up doing what job he or she normally does. He may call the person over to him and say, "I want you in the choir" or "Why aren't you up playing the guitar?" One of the few legitimate breaks in service occurs when the pastor himself "sits" someone down or after a marriage, a new baby, an illness, or an injury; otherwise, everyone in the church should have a job that they are to do cheerfully, as unto the Lord.

In a busy church like this one, for most people, the week is divided between the demands of full-time jobs, family and home life, frequent Saturday morning church meetings and functions (for example, the monthly Men's and

Women's Fellowship Breakfasts), occasional department meetings (also frequently held on Saturdays or Sundays between services), a Saturday night service, three services on Sunday, and a variety of special guest speakers, concerts, or other events during the week, and accompanying the pastor on his travels to other ministries as part of his busy itinerary. Members—particularly the singers and musicians and the ushers (Royal Guards), and the Security Ministry (bodyguards[1])—have to actually leave the church for a time in order to get a break from the dizzying round of activities that require their donated labor. Taught that God wants to do much to bless them financially and in every way, many of them allow themselves to become overworked and even neglect their families and other responsibilities *outside* of the church and its activities.

With the demands that members are encouraged to place on God they should be just as willing or more to give all that they have—including their time and talents—to God's work, running the church so that more souls can be saved just as theirs were. Selfishness is the charge leveled at those who appear to hold back on their contribution to this program. The boundary between church and the private lives of members must be drawn and maintained by the members themselves. The project of running a church with as large a social and spiritual vision as this one—a church that has "something going on every night," an often-heard description—could become a second full-time job for many people if they allowed it to. So it becomes imperative for members to learn to set boundaries, a concept that is not often talked about from the pulpit but that seemed to emerge in my conversations with members.

Not just a pew member, Cassandra has a job in the church: she works in the children's ministry. She volunteers as a Sunday school teacher, teaching the seven-year-olds' class. Before she injured her knee and had to take some time off to recover from her surgery, she would work with the children every Sunday morning, while their parents attended the eight o'clock service in the sanctuary. She worked with the children *every* Sunday and rarely, if ever, took time off. If there was a guest speaker at the church on a weeknight, she might (or might not) attend the meeting. I questioned her about how she managed to participate in church-related activities (including and beyond her Sunday school job) as well as maintain a life outside of church and its demands. Members are implicitly (as well as expressly) expected to "show up every time the doors are open" at the church. This message comes down directly from the pastor, who frequently states it very explicitly when addressing the congregation. Other members often use peer pressure or direct confrontation with members who are not working (either because they are not present on a particular day or service, or because they don't have a job in the ministry) to enforce the expectation and requirement of full participation on the part of all members of the ministry. I wanted to know how Cassandra balanced church demands with her outside life when she was working in the ministry. She responded:

> Because I've grown, I didn't allow other people to put pressure on me to be at the church every time the doors were open. Because I had a life outside of that. And sometimes I'd come home from work, and I didn't want to go there during the week, so I didn't— unless I was going to a meeting and coming back home. But I was able to not allow other people to put their stuff on me. To be able to set those boundaries—you want to be out there seven days a week, hey, go for it. But don't tell me I have to be out there seven days a week.

I then asked her how she managed to do this and whether she had found it difficult. Others I interviewed had spoken of their own difficulty (and that of others they knew) in negotiating the demands on their time and attention that other people in the ministry placed upon them. Cassandra said:

> Actually, it has become easier over time. Because when I go back, I'm going to limit *some more* time with folks! [laughing heartily] So it has become easier over time. Because I realize I have to take care of me. And I can't take care of everybody else and do everything for everybody else. And I don't feel a sense of guilt behind it—I don't feel like God's saying no, you *have* to be here every Sunday, every Wednesday, every Monday, Wednesday, and Friday for Intercessory Prayer. And so I think of myself and my relationship with God, and the way he is with *this* child, with *me*. So if other people don't like it, I don't care.

I encouraged her to elaborate on this point because there is great pressure put on people in the ministry to work in it and to show up for the many activities and events that are produced on a regular basis. I asked if she feels that pressure and what, if anything she does to deal with it:

> I used to. I used to because I was concerned with what other people thought. I didn't show up, what would they think? I don't *care*—I can actually say that now, and there was a time in my life where I couldn't.
>
> I think what's happened is that my *professional* self has gotten together with my Christian self, and some good things have come out of that—because the Bible doesn't really talk a lot about setting

boundaries—calling them "boundaries." I learned that in my profession. About setting boundaries. I tell clients all the time that they need to set boundaries. Well, how can I tell them that if I'm not setting boundaries in my own life with certain things? And so the combination of the two has caused me to grow in such a way where now I'm not concerned with what other people think. But, you know, sometimes it crosses my mind. *But not enough* to where I feel "Okay, I'm going to be out there seven days a week!" It's not gonna happen. And I'm okay with that.

Cassandra describes some of the strategies and tactics she has devised for negotiating the demands other people—including the pastor—would place on her time and her behavior as a member of the church. As a result of her knee injury, she took a break from working at the church to recover and to do some other things with her time. It might not seem unusual to take time off as a result of an injury or illness, but she also spoke of limiting more of her time when she returned to working in the ministry once she was more fully recovered from her surgery. Cassandra told me that one of her expected outcomes from taking more time away from working in the children's ministry at her church was that those who worked with her and supervised her, her colaborers, would see that they actually *could* make it without her, and that they would come to appreciate her in her absence. These things may appear contradictory, but in the context of a very demanding ministry in which every person's perceived lack of participation (especially when they have a specific job) is seen and read back to them as a sign of a lapse in their faithfulness, the pressure is great to think that each person is the only one who can do a certain job, and the demand is frequently made without any explicit expression of appreciation or gratitude. It is their service to the Lord, not to their coworkers or the church as organization.

Many times when they do show up and work, people are left feeling unappreciated, as they often do in their day-to-day secular job as well. Among those I interviewed, this theme was one of the most common. One way some members cope with their feelings of not being appreciated and valued as contributing their precious time (time that might just as easily be spent elsewhere) is to withdraw it for periods of time, taking sabbaticals.

Another way members negotiate the constant demands on their time is revealed very clearly by Cassandra in her discussion of boundary setting. This may seem to be out of the question for some church members, but, as Cassandra shared, she found it *essential* to preserve a sense of separation between the spheres of her life: church, work, and her personal life. That is not to say that she makes such distinctions in her own personal spiritual walk—she said that the integration of her education and professional life with her spiritual life enabled her to give church work a certain place, while still leaving room for other, non-church-related activities. In this way her horizons are broadened and her identity as an African American woman is no longer limited or put into a "box," as she describes it. That sense of empowerment also extends to her participation in the church. It is this boundary-setting practice that allows her to negotiate the demands of such a large and powerful ministry with its far-reaching and resource-intensive agenda.

For some people, the broadening of one's horizons and desires, as a result of believing and attempting to live out the teachings of the Faith Message, seems to engender a certain degree of tension. This tension arises when they are drawn away from expending their personal resources (time, talent, money, interest) on this particular church in order instead to fulfill or actualize themselves in other chosen paths and life and career goals. The pastor says to people (jokingly in the midst of services) that he will pray they will get a job in the area so they can stay and never have to move away from his church. In Cassandra's case, it was *both* her education and her understanding of what it means to know who she is in Christ that led her to realize the need to set some very real boundaries on the time she donated to the church (with, she felt, little appreciation).

This struggle for an identity and personal space apart from the church and church-approved (or sponsored) activities was experienced by other respondents, both male and female. One woman spoke of her desire to study dance and acting and to perform in local civic theater. As a member of the church's Theater Arts Ministry (TAM), she felt limited and constrained by the evangelical, dogmatic content of the productions. She was also uncomfortable with the limitations on using and expressing one's body in certain ways that some of those working alongside her (or, again, the pastor) might interpret as sexually suggestive or sensual and therefore inappropriate in a church setting, in the context of a theatrical production, a form of inspirational entertainment.

Thus "church member" is and should be thought of as a social role, carrying with it a whole host of expectations for appropriate behavior. Those expectations, or norms, are strictly enforced in a variety of ways, including pressure applied by other members as well as direct pronouncements of the leader, the pastor. For some people in the ministry, church—one's membership and the expectations and demands that flow from that social role—can also serve to put people (and God) into a box, which they then feel they must escape to make space for themselves to be individuals, as well as as members of a body. That is not to say that these parishioners do not want to serve their church or to give back to their community. That is far from the truth. In fact, they tend to be some of the most committed members; they just want to be able to achieve a sense of *balance* between the various other areas of life and the constant demands placed on them for their exclusive contribution of their time, talents, money, and allegiance to one institution, their local church.

They are not self-centered and unwilling to roll up their sleeves and work, as others in the church may label them. But they are also not content to spend every waking moment doing church-related activities. They want to achieve a state of dynamic balance and integration between the various spheres of their existence. Although the pastor and the Word of Faith Movement would impose on them an image of the church as the center of their Christian experience (and as symbolic of their primary identity as believers), these members seem to be struggling against and resisting such a *totalizing* conception of their membership in the ministry.

Leaving: When a "Break" Becomes Permanent

Finally, when members feel that, for whatever reason, they can no longer continue to attend the church, they decide it is time to move on and to leave the ministry altogether. For some people, the doctrinal demands, in addition to the demands placed on church members, become too much, and they begin to feel unable or unwilling to struggle to try to meet them any longer. Just as many members have switched from other churches or denominations, they also move back out of Word of Faith Movement ministries. Anecdotal evidence suggests that many of those who leave large Word of Faith Movement megachurches go to smaller churches.

Several people expressed dissatisfaction with their experiences in large Word of Faith Movement ministries and said that they had moved on to smaller, newer "Word" churches or gone back to denominational ones. One of the common reasons given was that they began to see through the movement's claims to be free from the types of traditionalism and legalism that they had been taught was the sole province of the denominational churches. One respondent, Charlene, said that positive confession seemed to her to be little more than a "word game" and that the ways of the Old Church Mothers in the Baptist church of her youth offered a sense of continuity with the past that is lacking in a movement that is always looking to provide the newest, the best, and the most ostentatious displays of its own grandeur and of how much it has progressed from those traditions.

Another respondent, Gerald, who had grown up in a denominational

church in the Apostolic (Holiness) denomination, had come to Faith Christian
Center in the late 1980s. He was a musician, and after a period of about five
to six years during which he played in the new ministry and was deeply involved there, he began to feel that it was becoming less of a place he could stay
and continue to grow spiritually. There were many reasons for his feelings and
subsequent decision to leave the ministry. In talking to him about his decision
to leave the ministry and the movement, I was also interested to learn how he
saw himself relative to the teachings that were so central to his spiritual self-
concept during the years he was in a Word if Faith Movement ministry. His
responses shed more light on the ways people use their understanding of
religion in their everyday experience:

> I still consider myself . . . Well, first of all I don't think that you can
> be in Christ and not be part of a faith move. Because, first of all, our
> whole background is faith, you know. That's what it stands for, you
> know, you're saved by grace through faith. Or whatever the quote is.
> I think all, from what I can gather from where I am now, a lot of the
> religions, sects or whatever you want to call them, have highlights.
> Some great points that are applicable and really have validity. But,
> however, I think there's things from all of them that you could really
> leave behind.

I asked if he meant all religions or Christian sects in particular. He replied:

> I can only speak to Christian because I don't know much about
> them and I can't do any detail on that. But from what I have been
> exposed to and what Christ taught openly, man will finagle what he
> wants in and, you know, leave out the other part that maybe can flip
> the whole puzzle. And then you've got this church over here saying
> this is the way to go, this is way God wants us to go. And then you
> have this other church saying, no. That's cool, but we found that
> this is it. And they're not putting it together and working out the
> differences. So for me right now I'm pretty much almost on neutral
> ground. Really. You know, because that keeps me from being cyni-
> cal. You know because I see on both sides from where I came from.
> That Apostolic thing which is bent on rules and legalities. You know,
> that was too much. And I don't believe that I was set free or I was
> enlightened spiritually for me to be put in bondage again. You know,
> at the same time I don't think God wants me so focused on being
> prosperous that I can't do the work of God, you know? I really don't.

He went on to say that although he no longer considers himself part of the Word of Faith Movement, he still believes in concepts he learned there, such as knowing who you are in Christ, that it is God's will for believers to be prosperous, and the practice of positive confession, among other things. So it appears that even though this man has left the movement, he does not leave as a blank slate—just as he did not come to the movement as a blank slate. He is taking with him lessons and insights gained as a member of Faith Christian Center to the next form of religion he accepts, and his reception of it will now be shaped by his experience growing up Apostolic and having spent years in the Word of Faith Movement. I also wanted to know what specific things started him on his transition out of the ministry as a member.

> Well, first of all I found that if you're not being involved the way the pastor wanted you to be involved, if you're not up in there spending all of your time, you know, and if you're about your own life then people tend to look at you like Well why aren't you doing what you used to do? Or I want you to be up in here. So that means, pretty much, it starts getting back to the same . . . Almost like the legalism that I saw when I was in the Apostolic church. And I have to give a little background because when I was going, when I first came to Christ I was in the Apostolic faith, I was in Bible Study Tuesday nights. I was at River Service on Thursday night. I was in choir rehearsal, Saturday. Sunday morning Sunday school. Eleven o'clock service, then six o'clock Young Peoples' meeting, 7:30 evening service. That was every week. For, gosh, from the early seventies 'til the early eighties.
>
> Yeah, pretty much we were there in the church. You know, like I said, when I got to Faith I was very leery about being involved in any kind of stuff. But then as I began to get into the music department then I found out that, okay, so now you need to be here on Tuesday. Here we go again. You're in the choir. Now you got to be here on whatever day—Thursday. And then it just got into that whole . . . it just went back into that ritual thing again.
>
> [The ritual of] being in the building, you know, whereas I believe—and this is me—I believe that *the church is the believers.* Not the building, you know. And there's people out on the streets that will never get to a building. And Christ wants us to be in the world and letting them see a light. How you gonna be a light amongst a whole bunch of lights? You know? It's kind of hard to do. If you're going to be somewhat of a beacon you need to be . . . where that

beacon can be seen: in the darkness or in the middle of all that confusion. So, my thing was getting out of there. Two. I started seeing that whole thing. I also started seeing "If you don't do as I [the pastor] want you to do, then you really ain't doing." "You're not doing" or "I'm not happy with you."

For instance, like being a part of the music department. When I saw [working in the ministry] was taking away from some other things I needed to do, especially after I got married, I wasn't able to do all that. So, you know, [the pastor] wasn't very pleased with that. Then, at the same time, you know, another thing that started me out was because, too, when [my wife] and I became engaged. First of all we dated without anybody really knowing that we were dating. Okay. Then when it was found out that we were engaged, and had not gone through the marital program, that counseling *thang*, you know, that was looked at as though, oh, you didn't go through the . . . you haven't done this . . . "Oh, you must not want your marriage to be blessed," or "Don't you want to be blessed?" And I'm sitting here looking at all these people who have been through all that junk and still wound up divorced. You know. So, I really . . . those are the kind of things that started weighing on my mind. You know. That I really don't want . . . I'm getting back into a ritual and I don't think God wants it to be a ritual. At least for me.

That you do certain things to be a part of this ministry. If you don't do them? Then you must not be a part of us. Get with it, or go on about your business. It's the same way with tithing. They're really strong on that tithing thing, and if you're not tithing *money* . . . "We want your money." And if you're not doing that, then they're looking at you crazy.

The arrogance that I saw in [the pastor] is a turnoff to me. Straight up, its a turnoff. Because, you know, I think to be a people person you really need to be amongst the people. You know, not be so far up that I can't touch you. You know, I've got to make so many appointments to get to, to get someone else. You know. You're not taking things personable [*sic*]. You're not taking them on a personal level any more. I understand that with the growth of the church you can't always get to everyone. But, however, it should be, you know, well thought of and have it situated where there are individuals that can really meet those needs and get to those people. Even with as much as [the pastor] has accomplished, and I think he's accomplished quite a bit in a short period of time, I really don't see him throwing much back into the community. I really don't. Maybe he is. I don't know. But I don't see it. Everything that I see is more self-gain. You know, *my* church, *my* members. You know.

So for Gerald his continued membership came to an end when the demands became greater than he was willing to give. Whether it was in terms of the amount of time he put in at the church as a musician or whether in terms of an uncritical stance toward the doctrine or even beginning to view the pastor negatively—whatever the issue, it was the fact that the church was not meeting his needs as a consumer of religion and of churches and the many forms of service they provide. Gerald has not completely thrown out the beliefs and teachings learned while in the movement. He says that he still believes in things like material prosperity being God's will for the believer and the like.

He also reveals a certain level of disenchantment with both the novelty of the message and with the charismatic personality of the leader, both of which figure prominently among the things that make this movement attractive in the first place. Respondents have said how they had never heard certain things before they came to a Word of Faith Movement church. They said that concepts like prosperity, knowing who you are in Christ, and positive confession were new to them when they were still in their denominational churches. But after some time has passed, as we see in Gerald's comments, the newness and the novelty begin to wear off, and the day-to-day role of being a church member begins to look and feel very similar to the way it felt back in the denominational church. So the grass really wasn't that much greener on the Faith side of the fence after all.

There are some people who, although their positions are supposed to be rotated so no one person ends up always being in a position like the one I just described, frequently find themselves part of the production of the service even when they are supposed to be off duty. They are unable to fully participate in the service the way they would if they were sitting in the audience with their family members instead of being up on the platform performing, or "ministering," as it is referred to in the church. This happens for a number of reasons, including the fact that there are some people who routinely fail to show up when it is their turn to work. It also happens because someone has an emergency or simply forgets (or doesn't know) that it is his or her week to serve. Some workers are more in demand by the pastor. Certain musicians tend to play in each service on Sunday (including the night service) because when they don't the pastor looks for them and questions why they aren't playing. Those members who are most "faithful" are often the ones to pick up the slack for the others, by virtue of the fact that they are always there in the services and willing to step in and help out.

The main concern of this chapter has been *how* members negotiate the great demands placed on them as part of membership in such a dynamic church; one whose ambitious leader has a vision to take the city, the state, and the country for Jesus. Members talked about their experiences as workers in the ministry and how they struggle to conform to the demands their social role as members placed upon their time, talents, attention, money, and any other resource they possessed that might be called into service to fulfill the pastor's God-given vision through the organizational medium of the church. Members also discussed how they struggle to maintain a life outside the walls of a church whose culture that can at times seem all-consuming and overwhelming.

The focus has been on how people "work out their own salvation" as they understand and have to live it. Contrary to the expectation that they accept and direct their conduct according to every new revelation of the pastor, they actively filter his messages, tailoring them to their individual or family situations. When confronted with a church culture that does not allow them to openly question or to challenge authority, they still manage to express themselves through venting networks. In the face of an implied and expressed expectation that they be at the church every time the doors open, and that they be always working and not just "sitting down" like some other members, they take breaks, sometimes for years, before returning to the ministry and to church service. And finally, when all these demands and expectations become more than they are willing to give, the break can become a permanent one, and they take their personal power back by leaving the ministry and taking the resources of their bodies, their time, their talents, and their money with them.

5

Prosperity in African American Religion

Thou shalt remember the Lord thy God: for it is he that giveth thee power to get wealth.

—Deuteronomy 8:18

"¡Yo quiero lo mío!" A young Hispanic woman unflinchingly demands. She seems to be looking right at me across the distance between her as a televised image and me as a bleary-eyed, early-Sunday-morning-before-church channel surfer. "I want my stuff—*RIGHT NOW!*" a professionally dressed African American man demands, bouncing boxer-style on his toes for extra emphasis. An African American woman signs the phrase with an intensity that mirrors that of the spoken words. So forcefully do they convey a sense of authority and *urgency* as they lay their claim to their "stuff" that I find myself caught up in the collective effervescence of the moment. It is all I can do to keep myself from adding mine to their chorus of voices "YEAH, I WANT *MY* STUFF RIGHT NOW, TOO!"

These are the opening moments of a commercial for the Faith teacher Creflo A. Dollar's videotape series *Laying Hold of Your Inheritance: Getting What's Rightfully Yours.* The spot continues with two short excerpts from this dynamic, African American minister's message to the believer. With great passion, his arms extended before him, he entreats the viewer: "God knows how to lay hold of the *invisible* until it becomes *visible*; all He wants us to do is be like Him!" In another clip he very animatedly, and with eyes wide, shouts in a rapid-fire cadence: "You already possess everything that you're trying to get ahold of. But we gotta learn how to *seize* it; *we gotta learn how to lay hold of the invisible!*" The voiceover continues: "Learn how to get what's rightfully yours with our monthly product offer *Laying Hold of Your Inheritance.* To order this powerful four-tape series, write to the address or call the number on the screen."

This advertisement for Pastor Dollar's tape series was aired at the end of the weekly broadcast of "Changing Your World," an outreach production of World Changers International Ministries. This is the 20,000-member, African American megachurch in College Park, Georgia, that was founded and is co-pastored by Dr. Creflo Dollar and his wife, Taffi. The ministry was one of several profiled in an *Ebony* magazine article on megachurches, with congregations of 10,000 to 25,000, in predominately African American communities across the country. On the morning I saw it, that 30-second television spot seemed to crystallize the spirit of the Word of Faith Movement.

Many of today's high-profile teachers of the Faith Message are well-dressed, energetic, and politically and financially savvy African American men, like Pastor Dollar, Pastor Fred Price of Crenshaw Christian Center in South Central Los Angeles, and Pastor Keith Butler of the Word of Faith International Christian Center in Southfield, Michigan. It would be inaccurate, however, to think of the Word of Faith as a *Black* religious movement. The movement has attracted followers from a broad demographic spectrum throughout the United States and in many countries abroad since its emergence in the 1960s and 1970s. This movement and its message have fired the imaginations and inspired the faith of thousands (and perhaps even *millions*) of followers the world over. Nevertheless, it is worth examining the implications, in the religious history of African Americans, of a movement that teaches that here and now is where God wishes to "prosper" the faithful. Today's movement may appear to be a new development to some observers, but the Word of Faith Movement actually stands in a long line of similar religious movements to emerge in twentieth-century America—movements that have synthesized New Thought metaphysics with evangelical, charismatic Christianity. As in today's Word of Faith Movement, African Americans have played a significant part in these earlier movements.

The religion and religious institutions of African slaves and their descendants in America have always had to be concerned with the material, social, political, and spiritual needs of their followers. To limit ministry to the spiritual realm was a luxury they could not afford, given the legacy of slavery and their post-Emancipation experience of discrimination. It was the role of Black churches and other religious institutions in their communities to take up the slack and meet the needs of the people. This must be appreciated to fully understand the movement under observation in this book.[1] Many in the Word of Faith Movement claim to possess some new revelation of God's divine plan, but in reality the Faith Message is not a body of new teachings, despite its differences from past prosperity teachings and movements.

Elder Lightfoot Solomon Michaux, "The Happy Am I Evangelist," was important in the history of urban religious movements with large African American followings. He was the founder of the Gospel Spreading Church and from the 1920s through the 1940s played a significant role not only in African American religion but in the early development of religious radio and television broadcasting. Under his leadership the church developed the 594-unit Mayfair Housing Project (in Washington, D.C.), whose "Mayfair Mansions" was one of the largest privately owned housing developments for African Americans in the United States and one of the first *church-related* housing projects back in 1946.[2]

Another leader of an urban religious movement with a sizeable African American clientele was the man born George Baker but better known as Father Major Jealous Divine, or "Father Divine." Father Divine established the Peace Mission Movement in Sayville, Long Island, New York, in 1919, during the height of the first great wave of African American migrants from the South to the northern urban, industrial centers like New York, Detroit, and Chicago.[3] Frequently mentioned in the same breath as Father Divine was Charles Manuel Grace, another of the flamboyant leaders of urban religious movements that gained a large African American following in the years immediately following the Great Migration. This charismatic leader—also referred to by many of his followers as "Sweet Daddy" Grace—founded the United House of Prayer for all Nations and promised his believers, mostly poor urban African Americans, that they could live the good life by placing their trust, their faith, and most of all their money in his hands. The organization owned a coffee plantation in Brazil and an egg hatchery in Cuba and was reported to own between 111 and 350 churches nationwide. Daddy Grace wore long hair and kept long fingernails and lived lavishly in mansions across the country owned by the organization. One of those was a 20-room mansion in Montclair, New Jersey, as well as an 83-room mansion on the West Coast. The number of his followers was estimated at between 27,500 and three million at various points over the course of his lifetime and ministry. He died in 1960.

From "Survival" to "Better Living" to "Prosperity":
African American Religious Materialism

Today's Faith Message is a synthesis of more than one belief system: one strand comes from contemporary evangelicalism's emphasis on the "born again" experience and on the inerrancy and absolute authority of the Bible in all matters; another part draws on the beliefs and practices of the charismatic movement's free operation of the gifts of the Spirit, based on the biblical account of the day of Pentecost in the book of Acts. However, it is its New Thought strand that promises believers prosperity and other earthly rewards if they will learn to apply certain principles in order to "real-ize" God in everyday life and situations. There is a strong practical, instrumental accent in New Thought metaphysical philosophies. Once believers learn to think, or "meditate," correctly (or "hygienically") and then speak accordingly, they have access to a power that comes directly from God and is made available to them as, at least in the case of the Word of Faith Movement, Christians through faith in Christ. But the emphasis placed on today's Faith teachers—for example, Frederick K. C. Price, who is thought to be responsible for bringing the Faith Message to the Black community[4]—neglects the historical context necessary to fully understand this particular movement and the development of its doctrine. Two people are responsible for introducing New Thought to the African American community through large ministries before today's Fred Price: Johnnie Colemon and Frederick Eikerenkoetter, better known as "Reverend Ike."[5]

Johnnie Colemon is the founder of the Universal Foundation for Better Living, an association of Black New Thought metaphysical congregations (especially those led by ministers trained at the Johnnie Colemon Institute, its educational arm). Colemon is an important, though little-known, figure in the development of African American New Thought institutions; she paved the way for the development of the Word of Faith Movement in the African American community. In 1956 she founded the Christ Unity Temple in Chicago, which was the first predominately Black Unity (New Thought) congregation. In 1974, having split with the Unity denomination in response to its pervasive racism, she founded the Christ Universal Temple for Better Living. She also established the Johnnie Colemon Institute, a school of metaphysics to educate and train ministers and lay people to carry the message of New Thought Christianity, based upon her teachings. The Universal Foundation for Better Living was incorporated as a New Thought denomination in 1974, with over 23 member congregations by the late 1980s. Colemon began broadcasting her messages on television in 1981, allowing her to reach a far larger audience than was possible preaching three services in her local church.[6]

Born and raised in the South, in her youth Colemon was diagnosed with an incurable disease. After reading some literature of the Unity School of Christianity, and practicing the teachings, which emphasized positive thinking to create healing and other manifestations of prosperity, she was disease free within two years. Today, Johnnie Colemon is still at the helm of the denomi- nation she founded back in 1956. Her foundation is the parent organization to a number of ministries, including what is said to be the largest metaphysical bookstore in the Midwest, the Colemon Academy elementary school, a multimedia center, restaurant and banquet facility, a prison ministry, and a 24-hour prayer ministry, to name but a few. Her church, which sits on a 32-acre "multicomplex" and reports serving nearly 20,000 members, is still spreading the gospel of living a better life through changing one's thoughts and speech to focus on positive things. Better living includes access to any and all forms of material, physical, social, and emotional prosperity. In some quarters Jonnie Colemon is known as "the First Lady of New Thought."

Colemon founded the first predominantly Black Unity congregation. New Thought metaphysical teachings, synthesized with charismatic Christianity, are the ideological basis for today's Word of Faith movement. Thus, Colemon should be thought of as a forerunner of the contemporary African American Faith teachers, although she is not generally thought of this way. Colemon's gender should not be overlooked. There are not many prominent African American women out front in the Word of Faith Movement. For the most part, the women who are visible generally play a secondary role as part of a ministry team headed by their husbands. It is likely that Colemon is not as well recognized as Fred Price or others of today's male Faith teachers because she was a church founder and pastor at a time when it was not generally acceptable for women to hold that office.

Another direct predecessor of the Word of Faith Movement in the African American community is the organization founded by Dr. Frederick J. Eikerenkoetter II, "Reverend Ike." The United Church and Science of Living Institute (founded in 1969) was preceded by the Miracle Temple in Boston, 1965; and Eikerenkoetter had founded another ministry in Harlem in 1966. He encouraged followers to seek the "good life" in the here and now, rather than waiting for their "pie in the sky" when they died. Like Johnnie Colemon, Reverend Ike built a church and an "institute" to teach people how to live better lives. Of course, the connotations of the word "better" suggest not only relationships and so forth but also living a life of material and physical abundance and prosperity. There are significant parallels to the Higher Life doctrine that informed Kenyon's doctrine.[7] Like the Faith teachers of today, Reverend Ike emphasized that God wanted believers to live "better lives" through the use of positive thinking. Like other "prosperity teachers" before him, Reverend Ike maintained a flamboyant lifestyle and spoke of poverty as a curse on humanity. Reverend Ike was well known for sayings such as "The best thing you can do for the poor is not become one of them" and "The *lack* of money is the root of all evil." He was also seen on television and was known for his "Blessing Plan," in which viewers became what are today referred to as "partners" with the ministry, financially supporting the production of the broadcast. This was not only a means of underwriting the broadcasts but was presented to the audience as a method for achieving one's financial goals and acting on one's faith, demonstrating that one desired and deserved financial prosperity and success. He would bless prayer cloths and send them to viewers in return for their financial donations. These cloths were supposed to have healing power and could be applied to the afflicted part of one's body to receive the benefit.

Like many other prosperity teachers and leaders of urban movements, Reverend Ike was not a native of Harlem, where his ministry rose to prominence. He was born in Ridgeland, South Carolina, in 1935 and later migrated north. He had graduated from the American Bible College in New York, earning a bachelor's of theology in 1956, and later served as a chaplain in the air force before returning home as an evangelist and faith healer. Back in Ridgeland, he established the United Church of Jesus Christ for All People in 1962 and the United Christian Evangelistic Association as its corporate vehicle. In 1964 he married and moved to Boston, where he established the Miracle Temple and his reputation as a healer grew. It was during this time in Boston that Reverend Ike began to teach about using the power of the mind to achieve prosperity.

Although they vary on a number of characteristics, a few things are common to each of these figures: (1) They all promised their followers, who were overwhelmingly from the poor and working classes of the Black community, the "good life" in this present world as well as in the next. (2) They incorporated New Thought metaphysics with the other teachings they espoused and disseminated to their audience; these ministries picked and chose (and mixed and matched) religious forms rather freely in times when this practice was not nearly as accepted as it is today. (3) They also spoke out against social injustice in various ways, including (but not limited to) direct or indirect participation in politics. (4) Finally, they extended their charisma into the realm of marketing products and diversified economic pursuits and utilized and appropriated the mass media in the service of their messages. In this respect, then, Elder Michaux, Johnnie Colemon, and Reverend Ike can be seen as direct predecessors of such notable African American television ministers as Frederick K. C. Price, Creflo A. Dollar, and T. D. Jakes.[8]

"Redefining Kingdom Business": Economic Development and the Contemporary Black Church

To varying degrees, economic activity and community development through their religious institutions has a long history in the experience of African Americans. Even so, there are many within the Word of Faith Movement who fail to acknowledge this long history of engagement with the material concerns of life from within a faith-based context. Moreover, despite the claims of many African Americans in today's movement that, historically, leaders of denominational Black churches have neglected to adequately empower and teach their members about financial matters—especially at the level of *personal* finance—indeed there *are* many denominational, non–Word of Faith ministries in which faith and economic development continue to mutually reinforce each other. Contrary to the claims of many of their members, Word churches are not the only ones in which remarkable examples of contemporary African American fiscal enterprise can be found.

In order to observe some of the more recent examples of the economic activity that has being conducted through or in connection with Black churches, one need look no further than the local communities in which these churches are situated and whose populations form the base of their clientele. Although mainstream American media may not be aware of it, the popular African American press has taken notice of, and is celebrating, the expansion of financial activity and community development within African American communities across the country. In the past five years several popular magazines have carried stories about the rise of Black churches involved in large-scale economic and community development, with or without the help of the federal government. To help situate the Word of Faith Movement's claim to leadership in financial matters in a broader context, the following section examines some examples of contemporary Christian economic activity in African American communities across the United States. What is significant in these ministries is, in contrast to that of some influential ministries of the past, the range and scope of these ministries' activities and the resources many of them have at their disposal. And although some are part of the Movement, many of these ministries do have denominational affiliations and are not related to the Word of Faith Movement in any way.

Christian Capitalism in the African American Community

Black Enterprise magazine ran an article entitled "Economic Deliverance through the Church" in its February 1997 issue in which the author says that "Black churches are bringing the gospel of economic development to inner city communities" and looks at a variety of projects successfully undertaken in recent years by prominent ministries led by African Americans, situated in inner-city communities with large African American populations, and concerned with not only saving souls but also providing jobs, addressing societal ills, and creating wealth in and for members of the African American community.[9]

One of these churches was Atlanta's Wheat Street Baptist Church, whose nonprofit organization, Wheat Street Charitable Foundation, serves the community as its development "arm." According to the article, the church takes in more than $50,000 in rents annually and has real estate holdings worth more than $33 million. Listed among Wheat Street's enterprises and holdings are its North and South Plazas, with two strip malls that house 10 small businesses (not owned by the church) on Auburn Avenue in the Martin Luther King, Jr., historical district; the Wheat Street Towers (a senior citizens' home); the Wheat Street Gardens (a low-income family housing development); and a 1,000-member credit union with assets of more than $1 million. The business manager, Eugene Jackson, explains that the church's former pastor, William Holmes Borders, Sr., provided the motivation and the vision for the church to move into the economic realm and take on the type of development projects that it has. Jackson said: "[Rev. Borders's] vision was to make religion pragmatic. It's not enough to have worship service on Sunday. The Church has to meet the needs of its members and their community."[10]

Another ministry discussed in the article is the 2,500-member Northwest Community Baptist church in Houston, Texas (pastored by James Wallace Edwin Dixon II). This church, whose annual budget was, at the time of the article's publication, $1.5 million (up from $50,000 16 years before), has constructed the 36,000-square-foot Excel-Eco Shopping Center, which also houses a number of small businesses. Among those businesses are the Deliverance Grocery and Deli Institute, a grocery store training initiative; a drug rehabilitation center; and 22.6 acres of land purchased in 1990 for $955,000, for the purpose of building a 3,000-seat sanctuary, community life center, and Christian educational facility. A nonprofit organization directs Northwest's economic activity: the Excel Eco Community Development Corporation played a key role in the negotiations to purchase the land. Out of this corporation developed the

Excel-Eco Construction Company, made up of a group of church members who were also builders. This company was contracted to renovate the site in preparation for the church's planned construction project. The construction company and other businesses owned or co-owned by the church as part of the Excel-Eco Shopping Center provide revenue for the church's other projects by tithing 10 percent of their profits as reinvestment back into the parent organization. The key to Northwest's success, according to the article, has been its savvy in negotiating the purchase of real estate.

Floyd Flake, the senior pastor of Allen African Methodist Episcopal Church in Queens, New York (and a member of the United States House of Representatives from January 1986 to December 1997), is quoted in the article as saying: "We've realized that the political-social model we've been operating on in the last 30 years is bankrupt." Apparently, what Flake meant in the statement was that the Black Church can no longer focus only on achieving social justice and political opportunity. This model has been eclipsed by post-civil-rights-era American economic realities, as the ranks of "The Truly Disadvantaged," or permanent underclass, have swelled in the 1980s and 1990s. The need for jobs and economic opportunity leading to financial stability and economic self-empowerment seems to be shaping the agenda of today's business-minded religious leaders in much the same way the structure of a Jim Crow society shaped the political activity of ministers only a generation or so ago.

The economic development activities of Flake's church focused on building an apartment complex for senior citizens with federal Housing and Urban Development (HUD) funding. It created the Allen Housing Development Fund Corporation, which came to own and manage a 300-unit housing development, as well as 10 other nonprofit organizations. These nonprofits provide a variety of community social services, including a resource center for battered women and a home care agency. The church-based organization also holds other real estate, as well as renovating buildings to rent space out to local businesses.

In 2002 South Central Los Angeles marked the tenth anniversary of the uprising and social unrest triggered by the trial in the Rodney King police beating. In response to the unrest in the area, exacerbated by the high rate of unemployment, the First AME Church, popularly known as "FAME," developed a community organization in 1992 to address the need to rebuild South Central Los Angeles and make it an economically viable community. The name given the organization was FAME Renaissance, and it includes approximately 13 different community services, one of which is the Business Resource Center. This center offers a revolving loan program for entrepreneurs interested in starting new businesses or expanding existing ones. The payments made on the loans go back into the loan program to help others in the same manner.

This is a modern-day mutual aid society, but in economic development terms; it is not just a food pantry, a clothes closet, or a provider of rent and bills assistance.

The article summarizes the ethos of "Christian capitalism" that is motivating Wheat Street and the other churches in their forays into contemporary forms of economic community development:

> This brand of Christian capitalism encourages African Americans to pool their dollars to invest in each other and their communities. Unlike a corporation that keeps its profits, church-based business enterprises enrich the neighborhood by providing resources and much needed services like day care, soup kitchens and substance abuse counseling.[11]

Out of the Church and into the Forum

The cover of the September/October 2000 issue of *Gospel Today* magazine carries the headline "Redefining Kingdom Business: Leading Ministries Shaking up the Economy"[12] and photos of two well-known African American ministers, both with very large congregations and, seemingly, an even broader range of business pursuits as heads of their respective ministries. These two men, Bishop T. D. Jakes and Pastor Kenneth Ulmer, are held up as examples of the ways African American Christians are branching out and expanding the boundaries of Christian ministry to include financial and economic stewardship of resources and community economic development.

According to the article, there is indeed a shift, or transfer, of wealth from the hands of the "sinner" (secular or "unsaved" individuals, organizations, etc.) to those of the "righteous," those to be found within the influence of the church and evangelical religious community. The introduction to the story tells its readers: "In case you haven't been paying attention, there is something huge going on in the area of 'prosperity' among Christians"[13] and goes on to profile the economic influence of several religious leaders in the communities in which they are situated.

Bishop Jakes (who was also featured on the cover of the July 2001 issue of *Time* as the year's "Best Preacher" and possibly the next Billy Graham) is the pastor of the Potter's House church in Dallas, Texas, and fast becoming a major figure in evangelical commerce. With more than 80,000 attendees, his yearly women's conference, "Woman, Thou Art Loosed," filled the Atlanta Dome in 2000 (as well as the Super Dome in New Orleans in 2001), and, without the help of the mayor's office, brought an estimated $100 million into the local economy of Atlanta via hotels, restaurants, and retail. After Graham, Jakes is reportedly the only other evangelist to bring this kind of attendance to such a large venue. He is also fast becoming a leader in the marketplace of "inspirational entertainment." In fact, Jakes is the prolific author of several Christian self-help books and a financially successful—and critically acclaimed—stage play, "Behind Closed Doors." If those enterprises were not enough, he has recently launched his own music record label, Dexterity Sounds, in collaboration with EMI Gospel Group, a nationally known gospel music company, and has not only produced recordings of his own church's mass choir but signed several top-selling gospel music artists. Jakes is quoted as saying that he believes it is his God-given charge to develop *all* his talents to their fullest potential; that includes those talents not directly related to preaching and running a successful local church.

Los Angeles's Great Western Forum was once the home of the Los Angeles Lakers basketball franchise. This 17,500-seat stadium has served the local community as the venue for sporting events and music concerts since 1967 when it was built, but the Forum now has a new owner, a new purpose, and a new role in the community. Since its sale in the year 2000 for the sum of $22.5 million,[14] the Forum has been the home of Faithful Central, another of the megachurches that have recently emerged in the African American religious community. Led by their pastor, Bishop Kenneth Ulmer, Faithful Central's purchase of the Forum was big news in the Black Church community and served as a powerful example of the direction the contemporary Black Church is taking nationally.

Another ministry exemplifying recent trends in Christian economic development is Florida's Redemptive Life Fellowship church, led by Harold C. Ray, presiding bishop over the Kingdom Dominion Church Fellowship, a consortium of churches in West Palm Beach.[15] Ray, a former attorney, is the head of the National Center for Faith-Based Initiatives (NCFBI), described as "a national collaboration of faith-based entities" whose aim is the elimination of "historic poverty and the dependency-inducing system." The strategy for achieving this goal is the development of "self-actualizing and self-sustaining community-based economics" in inner-city communities across the United States.[16]

Ray presides over a 12-member board of governors[17] who administer what are referred to as "regional embassies," each of which are staffed by accountants, economists, political analysts, and so on. The sphere of influence of this collaboration of ministries is estimated at 80 million people.[18] The organization's goal is to become a "one-stop center" for more than 50,000 churches looking to consolidate and maximize their financial resources. The staff of each regional embassy oversees economic development and funnels resources into the local communities and churches. Bishop Ray's future plans include the establishment of a National Faith-Based Law Center, a National Faith-Based Tax and Accounting Center, and a series of websites encouraging Blacks to invest, shop, financially plan, and make travel arrangements through their own local communities.

Ray was pictured on the cover of the July 2001 issue of *Gospel Today* magazine in a photo with President Bush. The president, in one of his first official acts in January 2001, created the White House Office of Faith-Based and Community Initiatives by executive order. The mission of the Office is to lead a "determined attack on need" in American communities. The program was designed to provide federal funding that would allow the role of faith-based community organizations to be expanded and strengthened so they might be able to compete with other social service groups and provide services to the needy through government or privately funded sources. To help promote and implement his faith-based initiative plan, the president created the Centers for Faith-Based and Community Initiatives through another executive order. These centers are attached to seven cabinet departments: Justice, Agriculture, Labor, Health and Human Services, Housing and Urban Development, Education, and the Agency for International Development. The intent of the president's program is to use government to help and not hinder faith-based community groups, building on the types of organizations that have long existed in the African American and many other communities. It also gives official recognition to the important role these organizations have played in the lives of those who have been involved with them.

One final example of contemporary African American faith-based organizations in community development and wealth creation is the Nehemiah Corporation of America, a not-for-profit community development corporation whose approach to community development and revitalization takes the form of economic empowerment and wealth creation prinicipally through home-ownership and affordable housing. This faith-based organization was first established in Sacramento, California, in 1994, and since 1997 the flagship Nehemiah Program has grown to become the largest privately funded down payment assistance program nationwide. The corporation's subdivisions include: the Nehemiah Community Reinvestment Fund, a financial institution specializing in financing community development projects; the Nehemiah Community Foundation, which supports other faith-based and community-based organizations; the Nehemiah Urban Christian Ministries Initiative, responsible for developing, sponsoring, and promoting new urban Christian ministries; the Sacramento Valley Fund, which invests in the development of housing, commercial, and industrial projects; and the Nehemiah Progressive Housing Development Corporation, which develops affordable housing for families and seniors through state and federal tax credit programs.[19] The thousands of new homeowners (from all racial and ethnic backgrounds), the new urban ministries begun and supported, the various community service organizations supported, and the community development and revitalization projects that have been funded through the Nehemiah Corporation of America and the other organizations discussed in this chapter all bear witness to the fact that today's African American faith-based organizations are continuing a tradition of economic investment and development in Black communities across the country.

The Black Megachurches

Another recent article, "The New Megachurches: Huge Congregations with Spectacular Structures Spread across the U.S.," profiled 16 churches described as "representative examples of a new trend in Black America that has caused conversions, talk and some controversy from Los Angeles to Atlanta and from New York to New Orleans."[20] The article classifies as megachurches those that have congregations of 10,000 to 25,000 members and are housed in spectacular buildings on large campuses.

The first of the Black megachurches profiled in the article is the Word of Faith International Christian Center in Southfield, Michigan. Founded in 1979 by Keith A. Butler and his wife, Deborah, this ministry was originally housed in a storefront building, which is how many urban churches began. Although the founding membership was only 60, today the church boasts an international outreach, with over 18,000 members and a 5,000-seat sanctuary on 110 acres of land just outside of Detroit. In addition to the church itself the campus includes the Bible Training Center, the Faith Christian Academy—enrolling children from preschool through high school—and the Kingdom Business Association, where Christian businesspeople learn to incorporate Christian principles in business operations. Also offered are specialized ministries for children, married couples, singles, men and women, and a music ministry. The international reach of the ministry is evident in the number of churches that have been founded overseas by Butler and his wife, Deborah L. Butler, who is a licensed, ordained minister in the church (their son is co-pastor with his father). They have founded 65 churches in Africa, 15 in Pakistan, and 2 in Bulgaria and Hungary, and they plan to open a new church in England. This ministry is actually part of the Word of Faith Movement, as its name clearly indicates.

Another Black megachurch is located in Houston, Texas. Pastored by Ira V. Hilliard, the New Light Christian Center began with 23 members but now reports a membership of 20,000. This church has twin campuses at identical North and South locations. Both had 5,000-seat arenas under construction at the time of the article. Pastor Hilliard, as part of the new breed of evangelical minister, travels by helicopter to deliver sermons at both locations each Sunday. This ministry also maintains extension churches in two other Texas cities.

Probably the most widely recognized figure in the Word of Faith Movement is Frederick K. C. Price, the pastor and founder of the Crenshaw Christian Center in South Central Los Angeles. The church's sanctuary, the 10,000-seat geodesic dome known as the "Faith Dome," is one of the largest church structures in the world, and street signs lead visitors to the church from the freeway to the impressive monument located on the campus formerly occupied by Pepperdine University. The Encyclopedia of African American Religions[21] credits Price with being the man who brought the Faith Message to the African American Christian community, and his stature is underscored by some who refer to him as the "godfather" of the Prosperity movement among African Americans. Crenshaw Christian Center was founded in 1973 with about 300 members. At present the membership is being reported as between 16,000 and 20,000. The ministry includes television, radio, book publishing, and tape distribution divisions. To date, 116 television stations and 42 radio stations carry the broadcasts from Crenshaw Christian Center. The ministry also publishes the quarterly magazine Ever Increasing Faith Messenger. Other ministries under Price's leadership include the Crenshaw Christian Center Ministry Training Institute (opened in 1985), the Correspondence School Program (1994), a preschool and elementary, junior, and senior high schools, a prison outreach ministry, and over 17 helps ministry auxiliaries and organizations, with approximately 1,500 volunteer workers. The ministry has over 311 paid employees working within 14 divisions of this massive and extensive organizational structure.

At the time of this writing, Crenshaw Christian Center is poised to become one of the first Word of Faith Movement ministries with a bicoastal presence. On March 27, 2004, a New York Times article reported the pending negotiations in which the ministry planned to purchase the historic First Church of Christ, Scientist, for $14 million dollars (incidentally, the price paid for the church's current Los Angeles property in 1981).[22] The new church building is located at the prestigious location of Central Park West and Ninety-Sixth Street in New York City, and it symbolizes the movement's emphasis on church growth, expansiveness, and the display of material prosperity. Since 2002, Price's ministry has been renting the facility, and he has held weekly Bible studies at the location as part of the process of establishing a new sister congregation to the one in Los Angeles. The congregation, which already has more than 600 members, is led by one of Price's assistant pastors, installed in position in 2003. The move to purchase the 2,200-seat, turn-of-the-century landmark structure and establish a permanent presence in New York City represents a major development in the ongoing expansion of the Word of Faith Movement by a man and ministry that have come to be synonymous with the movement, especially among its African American members. This new congregation and its stately facility should be seen as signaling the ongoing expansion of the African American megachurch phenomenon in general and the bicoastal expansion of the Word of Faith Movement—both frequently proceeding unnoticed by mainstream media. These trends in African American religion bear close observation as they develop into the future.

The Black megachurches discussed here are providing services to their members as well as the surrounding community. Their activities extend beyond basic pastoral care or attending to the needs of the spirit and soul. They are also working for economic development and financial empowerment in the inner city, rather than relying solely on government programs and administration. Today's Black ministers are decidedly entrepreneurial and well educated, with a staff of well-trained specialists in finance, accounting, economics, and community development, and they have access to resources that half a century ago were uncommon for many churches, especially those in African American urban communities. They are well connected, and they are among the first generations to directly benefit from the political and economic gains won in the civil rights movement. Bishop Harold Ray's NCFBI is an example of the ways Black churches across the country are transcending traditional denominational boundaries and barriers to unite for the task of making social change through economic development in communities where large numbers of African Americans live.

African American religion and religious institutions have always had to attend to the material conditions of life, as well as addressing spiritual issues. From the very beginning of the African presence in the Americas, they were circumscribed by the dictates of racism and discrimination and denied full and equal access to societal resources. Their religion spoke to that inequality and promised them resolution (or divine judgment in the future for the guilty). Some of the churches highlighted in this chapter are part of the Word of Faith Movement, and some are not. But they share certain characteristics: they are large ministries, offering a diverse and extensive array of services to their members and the surrounding community; economic development is an important aspect of their work; they use the mass media and other less traditional means of spreading the gospel. Most important, these are all churches led by African Americans.

Today's Word of Faith Movement markets itself as both a new revelation and an improved form of Christianity relative to what its members claim is being taught in more doctrinally traditional denominational churches, especially those in the African American communities. But this movement draws upon previous movements, trends, traditions, and streams of thought that preceded it in African American religious history. Religion and the resources of religious organizations have always played a major role in the economic survival and development of the African American community. The Word of Faith movement draws upon a long tradition of self-help and mutual aid, undergirded by an unapologetic religious sensibility. It is not new to teach people that it is not God's will for them to suffer from the poverty and lack that result from being effectively cut off from access to societal resources. It is another thing altogether, however, to teach that every one of them is destined to become wealthy if he or she would only change his or her way of thinking. But even that doctrine has its antecedents, which many members of today's Word of Faith Movement seem unwilling to acknowledge.

Conclusion

The word is nigh thee, even in thy mouth, and in thine heart: That
is, the Word of Faith, which we preach: That if thou shalt confess
with thy Mouth the lord Jesus, and shalt believe in thine heart that
God hath raised him from the dead, thou shalt be saved.

—Romans 10:6–10

This book has examined today's Word of Faith Movement, a distinct
subculture within the larger world of charismatic Christianity. Its basic characteristics can best be understood in terms of the doctrine
and the structure of the movement, and how the movement both resembles and differs from other forms of contemporary Christian belief, practice, and ecclesiastical structure. This movement is fiercely
nondenominational, and after nearly four decades of existence has
not developed an overarching jurisdictional or hierarchical body to
which member churches must be accountable. The primary organizational form of the movement is the voluntary association or fellowship that allows members of congregation and the ministers
leading them to join together in a relational community across this
country and even internationally.

Members of the network interact on the basis of their shared
understanding and acceptance of the basic tenets of the Faith Message. The Faith Message is characterized by the synthesis of elements of a number of previously existing doctrines and philosophical systems. It teaches that born-again Christians have direct access

to the mind of God through scripture and that, as long as they will apply the corresponding principles found in scripture, they can have divine health and material wealth in the present world in addition to heaven in the next. The Word of Faith Movement places great emphasis on the *rewards* of being a born-again Christian, and health and wealth are part of the "rights and privileges" that come from being saved and knowing who you are in Christ. The Faith Message is a *practical* and instrumental form of religion that purports to take complex points of theological debate and reduce them to elements that can and will work for any persons with enough faith to appropriate them—to name and claim them—for themselves. But what can we identify as the overall meaning of this movement and the doctrine that has captivated so many believers? There are several meanings.

Meanings of the Faith Message and the Movement

The Faith Message and Social Class

The Faith Message is a commentary on the socioeconomic stratification of Western capitalist societies, particularly America. It is a religious response to class hierarchy appealing to many who have traditionally been farthest from its center. By embracing the notion that poverty is a "curse" with a spiritual origin and affirming that prosperity is attainable and accessible to *anyone* who would only apply certain immutable laws, or the "formula," the Message challenges the limitations imposed by socioeconomic location at the same time that it "sanctifies" the attainment of wealth by those who have done so. I have shown the importance of class background in the stories of both Kenyon and Hagin, who were born essentially poor and attained limited formal education at best yet aspired to lives that transcended those barriers placed in their lives by accidents of birth. The Faith Message resonates for people who aspire to be successful, to be wealthy, and to have a life in which their health and general well-being are assured and protected by God. Followers are taught that this assurance, this "divine security," as it were, will be their reward for their faithfulness to God, their thinking the right thoughts and saying the right words, and their living a life of holiness. These things are all within the power of even the poorest, least-educated person to do, and success, material wealth, and self-fulfillment become much more accessible.

From this perspective, the Faith Message informs what might be seen (at least in part) as a type of "poor people's movement." The people who are its followers are primarily those whose experience has produced the *desire* for, if not the actualization of, upward socioeconomic mobility. This "faith formula for success" is a way of using religious doctrine to symbolically and supernaturally level the playing field with respect to access to society's resources. Since humans have constructed systematic barriers to opportunity and upward mobility, the Faith Message offers a way around those barriers by giving the believer *access* to societal rewards through a higher authority and a supernatural source of power. They see themselves as favored by God, who has promised them *every* good thing that their social class position might preclude, including money, health, and success, as part and parcel of their "rights and privileges" as believers. There is a tacit acknowledgement of the socially constructed nature of systematic inequality and social structure, but the doctrine teaches that faith in God renders those structures powerless to hinder the divinely appointed upward mobility of the believer. The curse of poverty (as a result of wrong thinking, sin, or confessing negative outcomes) has weakened those who do not rise, rendering *those individuals* themselves powerless over their own circumstances.

While it may give the impression of being a social movement attempting to bring about a more just society, a distinction should be made between the Word of Faith Movement and some other religiously informed movements for social justice. The Faith Message encourages *individuals* to be successful *within* the existing economic and social system rather than seeking to overthrow it or necessarily to reform it to any great degree. Those in the Word of Faith Movement frequently criticize those they consider to be part of the religious establishment, who are seminary trained or have other forms of formal education. These people are contrasted with many of the Faith teachers, who attended Bible colleges like those set up by Kenyon and Hagin, the primary goal of which is to produce new ministers or missionaries as quickly as possible. Their curricula include only what they deem absolutely necessary to go out and start a church or go into the mission field. The perspective and theological positions of those who have been trained for ministerial service in a vocational Bible training college are held up as superior to those of clergy with an academic background and training in a graduate theological seminary.

Prominent Faith teachers frequently caricature people with higher levels of education, particularly those who dispute or even question the orthodoxy of the Faith Message. Their educational level (as expressed in formal degrees) and the fact that they studied at an institution tied to a denominational body are pointed to as the reason they don't understand what the Bible "really" says concerning prosperity or some other point of doctrine that the Word of Faith Movement holds dear. Faith teachers often appear to criticize certain aspects of capitalism as an economic system—and the *nonbelievers* who prosper within it—while simultaneously praying and "confessing" that they are becoming one of those who also prosper within the same system. They do not oppose the system per se; rather, they do challenge their members' past or present marginalization from its center. The doctrine teaches (and I have personally heard more than one Faith teacher say): "The best thing we can do for the poor is not join their ranks."

While it may appear to be critical of the inequalities in the distribution of societal resources, what the Faith Message actually calls for is a redistribution of wealth out of the hands of "sinners" into the hands of born-again *Christians,* while preserving the system and its inequalities intact. It affirms the notion that America is basically a meritocracy, and where it does not operate as such in the lives of unfortunate or "cursed" individuals, the power of God can and does bridge the gap to believers' sharing in the rewards of living in a society with so much wealth. In the end, those believers who have prospered within the existing economic system have the reassurance that it is God's will for them to be where they are.

One final word about the Faith Message and social class bears mentioning. Many of the primary organizations and largest congregations within the movement were established or saw phenomenal growth during the decade of the 1980s. It is important to contextualize the growth and expansion of the movement at this particular historical moment and understand it in terms of shifts in American society set in motion by the presidential administration of Ronald Reagan (and later carried into the Bush administration). Reagan's conservative economic policies, "Reaganomics"—a central tenet of which was based on supply-side economic theory, or what critics refer to as "trickle-down" theory— resulted in a class structure that can be characterized by its simultaneous expansion of opportunity and financial prosperity for individuals and families among the highest strata (e.g., reforms reducing the tax rate for the wealthiest tier of taxpayers), coupled with a contraction of opportunities and financial stability for those individuals and families among the lowest strata (e.g., cutting or completely eliminating certain social programs from the federal budget). During Reagan's tenure as president the ranks of the homeless swelled, and a seemingly permanent underclass emerged, to become symbolic of what many still recall as a time when "the rich got richer and the poor got poorer."

But the harsh realities of Reagan-era economic policies for the nation's most vulnerable were very different from what was being portrayed of American life by the mass entertainment media. Popular culture of the time seemed to be shaped by the mass media producers' obsession with glorifying consumption through many highly successful television programs. Examples include shows like *Lifestyles of the Rich and Famous, Dynasty, Dallas, Falcon Crest,* and *Miami Vice.* Also heavily represented and marketed in the mass media were "designer" products like jeans, polo shirts, shoes, eyewear, and a whole host of other formerly "everyday" items and personal care products that promised a vicarious experience of wealth, accessible to a broad range of consumers. The popular culture of the decade emphasized extravagant—even opulent—self-indulgence and conspicuous consumption and was reflected in the content of many forms of mass entertainment. Images of American wealth fanned the flames of desire for prosperity, or at least the trappings associated with status, at the same time that millions of people found it increasingly difficult to secure affordable housing for themselves or their families.

Among the plethora of offerings of 1980s prime-time television, *The Cosby Show*, in which a successful, middle-class, Black, nuclear family was portrayed in a positive light, was extremely popular with Americans from a wide range of backgrounds. The "Cosby" family was appropriated as a symbol for many people (especially conservatives) that the experience of African Americans had been one of socioeconomic upward mobility and middle-class assimilation since the end, and as a direct result, of the Civil Rights Movement. The show presented a picture of a middle-class lifestyle and made it appear attainable to all, even African Americans.

But the reality of life in many African American families belied the Reagan administration's claims and the entertainment and advertising media's images of unbridled upward mobility and access to wealth and prosperity for all who worked hard (or who had sense enough to be born into the right families). Into this breach, this rupture, came today's Faith Message, like other prosperity movements of the past, offering a shining hope and an answer to the question why some people (especially born-again Christians) were not prospering in the midst of so much wealth. The answer was that those people had not been taught what the Bible really says about wealth and who should possess it. What appeared to be impossible through mere hard work and the secular opportunity structure God's favor could make possible for believers who know who they are in Christ.

The decade of the 1980s is an important moment in the development of the Word of Faith Movement and the spread of its message. During this time the movement that had begun in the late 1960s and early 1970s gathered steam and took on a momentum that would carry it through the next decade and into a new millennium. Some of the largest and wealthiest ministers and congregations within the movement taught that through believers' giving of money to the church (or, more accurately to God *through* the church) they were virtually guaranteed prosperity in return. Many who aspired to lifestyles of financial prosperity, or at least *stability* in an unstable economic climate, responded. As a result, these ministers and congregations amassed levels of wealth that allowed them to build, or prepare to build, the massive physical structures and educational, outreach, and broadcast facilities that then set the stage for and supported their further development into the megachurches that stand today. These are the churches that continue to disseminate the gospel of socioeconomic mobility that is the Faith Message. Despite evidence to the contrary, in the 1980s it appeared to many Christians that great wealth was available to all. They believed that government economic policies would not only benefit the top tier of the nation's families, based upon the Faith Message's promise. The promise was that if born-again Christians—as God's modern-day "chosen people"—would but exercise the power inherent in their faith to "name it and claim it," then whatever they wanted would be theirs, regardless of social class, level of education, family background, or any such measure of power, wealth, or prestige devised by human will.

The Faith Message in African American Religious History

When placed in the context of other prosperity movements in African American religious history, other insights into the Word of Faith Movement begin to emerge. For generations of its disenfranchised members, the Black Church had to attend to the material as well as the spiritual, political, social, and cultural issues affecting the lives of African Americans. Traditional mainline Black churches, along with those groups and movements that might be considered marginal, have *had* to meet the needs of African Americans through the formation of mutual aid societies and other cooperative forms of resource mobilization. Not only Christian churches have attended to the material needs of the African American; groups like the Nation of Islam have also maintained a strong ethic of economic self-help and mutual aid within the Black community. That ethic of survival was coupled with an emphasis on the spiritual as a necessary means to that end. Within the Black community in general, the spiritual has never been very far removed from material considerations. This was the direct result of the experience and status of African Americans relative to other racial and ethnic groups in the United States.

In light of the role of the traditionally close relationship between spiritual and material matters, there is another possible reading of today's Word of Faith Movement, one that situates it squarely within the context of African American religious history. Today's movement is but one more prosperity movement in a long line, dating back to the early part of the twentieth century. Large numbers of Blacks migrated from the rural South to the urban northern (and southern) centers seeking better opportunities and relief from the oppressive Jim Crow system. The alienation and disillusionment that met them in the "promised land" of cities like Chicago, Detroit, and New York gave rise to a number of religious movements responding to the once-again second-class economic status of Blacks in these new settings.

To one degree or another, movements led by such charismatic figures as Daddy Grace and Father Divine (during the Great Depression), Reverend Ike (during the 1960s and 1970s), Johnnie Colemon (founder of the Universal Foundation for Better Living, 1974), and even the Church of Hakeem (founded in 1978), all appropriated New Thought metaphysics and synthesized it with other forms of spirituality. The core of this philosophy teaches that thought, or "mind," is the source of all that comes into existence as "reality," even at the level of the individual believer. If followers would just change their way of thinking, these ministers taught, their objective circumstances would change to follow suit. According to this logic, poverty was essentially the direct result of a "poverty mentality." If they would take on a "prosperity mentality," then material prosperity would be the result. As I have shown, this is what today's Word of Faith Movement teachers are teaching.

This is not to say that all of these movements' teachings or emphases were identical; however, while these ways of thinking may appear new to some observers, looking even briefly at the record of African American religion we can see that there have been many predecessors to today's Word of Faith Movement and its teachers. Particularly for its African American members, the Word of Faith Movement draws on a long tradition in African American religion, with respect to the close relationship between the sacred and the profane. It does not represent something new.

The Word of Faith Movement as Contemporary American Religion

Several observers of contemporary religion have noticed the trend toward the evangelical megachurch. Kimon Howland Sargeant's book *Seeker Churches* (2000) described such churches, noting that they eschew denominational labels, embrace contemporary "praise and worship" musical styles, emphasize timely, "relevant messages," and offer a wide variety of goods and, most important, *social services* to meet the perceived and expressed needs of their members. These churches focus on attracting those who are seeking direction in their spiritual lives but who may be reluctant to commit to church membership because of negative past experiences or preconceptions. Others have looked at ways these so-called new paradigm churches are actually reinventing American Protestantism.[1] The congregation at Willow Creek Community Church is frequently cited as exemplary of this particular trend in contemporary American evangelicalism.

But these studies all tend to focus on congregations that are largely white and ignore this phenomenon as it has unfolded in the African American Christian community. Some of the largest and most economically diverse faith-based business enterprises, exactly what many of these ministries are, can be found in predominately African American communities and are led by African American ministers who are also savvy businesspeople. The reach of the Black Church into the mainstream business world is apparent in a number of diverse and lucrative business ventures beyond mere televangelism and the publishing of religious tracts. These enterprises include Christian or "inspirational" entertainment (the recording and movie industries, live theater, book publishing), investment, and the financing of small businesses. In short, many Black churches are no longer just eking out a meager existence—not just selling "chicken dinners"—but are owners and operators of restaurants and other nonreligious businesses that provide jobs in the communities where their churches are located and where their members live and work.

Churches within today's Word of Faith Movement share some characteristics with what are known as "seeker-sensitive" or "seeker" churches. Like a number of other currents in contemporary religion, the Seeker Movement is similar to the Word of Faith Movement in that it has not been formalized into a centralized organizational structure. Rather, it crosses denominational boundaries and is more aptly described as a network of churches with any number of denominational affiliations that have in common the following general tendencies. There is a desire to reach out to and evangelize those in the "unchurched" segment of society, particularly those who are turned off by traditional Christianity, for whatever reason. These churches attempt to draw those potential new converts and church members, the "seekers," into their congregations by demonstrating to them that religion and participation in a Christian community of faith can be "relevant," beneficial, and personally fulfilling.

The methodologies employed in these outreach efforts are tailored to the needs and cultural values of the target audience. Seeker churches use contemporary praise and worship music, offer a wide variety of self-help classes and support groups (with a therapeutic, personal fulfillment emphasis), social and even health services, youth groups, singles' ministries, men's and women's classes, and marriage and parenting classes; incorporate multimedia presentations into services; and give their churches "nonthreatening" names, architecture, and decor.

These largely suburban megachurches—some of them like miniature cities—tend to have a younger congregation than many of the mainline Protestant denominational churches, with Baby Boomers and their children making up the majority of the leadership and the laity. The conservative core of the traditional evangelical message is not being altered. But what is being changed is the packaging and delivery, which are shaped to resonate with the experience and expectations of contemporary people who think that a traditional, evangelical Christian message does not and *cannot* speak to them or their circumstances in today's complex world. Seeker churches attempt to deliver a traditional message in a nontraditional way.

The seeker movement is yet another example of the types of contemporary religious expression today that are a direct result of the transformations wrought by the Baby Boomers and the values that social scientists commonly associate with them. They prefer a decentralized organizational structure, and their "engaged orthodoxy"[2] allows them, like other evangelicals, to freely pick and choose certain elements from secular culture to incorporate into their belief system and practices. The traditional, politically conservative message is packaged in such a way as to make it more palatable to contemporary mainstream sensibilities. These churches also represent an expression of the therapeutic, voluntaristic, self-fulfillment ethic that has become so pervasive in American culture and has been an especially transformative agent in the way religion is being done. People's attention, their allegiance, their time and money are sought after and competed for by an ever-expanding array of entertainment and leisure options, computer games, the internet, and more. In this climate the use of secular marketing techniques to help "sell" religion is not only acceptable but also seemingly necessary.

In many ways Faith Christian Center resembles a seeker church: its name was chosen by the founder to be "nonthreatening"; the church building lacks steeples, spires, or anything else associated with traditional church architecture; it displays no anthropomorphic images of deity; its doctrine, the Faith Message, is one of personal fulfillment, and the church offers a wide variety of programs to its members and the surrounding community; it offers a practical, results-driven theology; it uses contemporary music, dance, music videos, short skits, and full-length theatrical productions in services, borrowing heavily from secular popular culture to help make newcomers feel comfortable enough to relax and listen to a very politically conservative, basically traditional evangelical message. A big difference between this megachurch and those reviewed in Sargeant's study is that it is an urban church with a predominantly African American, working-class clientele. It appears to have been missed in many of the discussions of the megachurch phenomenon. Thus the seeker movement may actually include many more ministries and members than previously realized.

The Faith Message as Ideology of Transition

Of all the possible readings of the Word of Faith Movement and its doctrine offered thus far, none is more compelling than the idea that at its very essence, the Faith Message operates in the lives of its followers as an ideology of socioeconomic transition.[3] It is a doctrine that gives ultimate significance to *movement* and *change*. As has been shown in the accounts of many of the people interviewed in this book, the Faith Message provides a religious and spiritual framework by which they might make sense of the changes that either have already occurred in their lives, those they desire, and those toward which they are striving.

The Old Testament provides an abundance of stories that may be (and are) appropriated as transition ideologies. For example, the book of Genesis teaches that God instructed Abram to pick up and leave his familiar surroundings—which included his extended family—and emigrate to a foreign country, a place where God would later change his name to "Abraham" and bless him materially, establishing everlasting covenant with him and with the descendants that God would also eventually provide. Similarly the Exodus story has fired the imaginations and inspired hope in believers for generations. The Exodus might be thought of as another Old Testament account appropriated as an ideology of transition, especially when understood metaphorically and mythically. This biblical account of God's intervention in the social and *material* condition of his chosen people, moving them from "bondage"—according to the Faith Message, symbolizing poverty, ignorance, sickness, and so on—to a "land flowing with milk and honey," symbolic of prosperity. Drawing upon this idea, the Faith Message teaches believers that, just as he brought the children of Israel to a place where he would bless them, God desires to move, to "deliver," today's faithful to new places where he will bless them and meet all of their needs and desires. This belief system provides an overarching narrative by which people are able to articulate this aspiration in spiritual and religious terms, rather than in secular terms. For many years traditional Holiness-Pentecostal thought held that the pursuit of worldly power, wealth, and prestige was antithetical to living lives of holiness, and it is from this background that a large portion of this movement's membership has switched their affiliations.

Perhaps most important in understanding the Faith Message as an ideology of transition is the fact that its power and resonance are not dependent upon its followers' actual *attainment* of material prosperity. Rather it is the pursuit of it, the *process* by which one yearns for and then works toward achieving, through faith, self-improvement and self-actualization with tangible results to follow. As an ideology of socioeconomic transition, this is where the doctrine draws its authority in the lives of believers. In this book we heard from people who almost all said they came to follow the Faith Message teachings because they were unsatisfied with what they had in their prior religious experience. They said they wanted *more* from their faith, not just that they wanted something different. The Word of Faith Movement is a fellowship of people who claim that they have been given more or are in pursuit of more, and that it is God's will that they should have it. Most of the people interviewed had indeed progressed socioeconomically, or were actively in pursuit of such progress. It might seem obvious to consider the need for a doctrine that would help those who had moved from one geographical location to another to provide some sense of ultimate meaning and transcendent continuity as they sought to reestablish themselves in a new and foreign place. But it is just as important for people who have moved from one socioeconomic level to another to be able to draw upon some form of ideology that helps make sense of the experiences and issues their new status presents to them or that they now have access to.

For many who have come from lower class positions than they now occupy, the Word of Faith church services, in addition to the doctrine, helps provide some sense of cultural continuity that might be lacking in other realms of their present experience. The Movement's emphasis on teaching versus preaching, in which a certain level of so-called middle-class decorum is expected, would have certain implications for people who may have been accustomed to Holiness-Pentecostal church services in which freedom of emotional display and ecstatic forms of expression are more highly valued. Because the Word of Faith Movement churches are charismatic in orientation, these new churches still allow expressions of religious ecstasy, but in a much more controlled manner. The emphasis on teaching and decorum would parallel members' current educational and career experience or aspirations, while still allowing space to just "have church" the way their parents' or grandparents' generation of Pentecostals did.

Regardless of the tradition, religion always exists in conversation with the larger cultural currents in the societies in which it is embedded and of which it is in part constitutive. It is shaped by the particular historical moment in which it lives, moves, and has its being. The Faith Message is no exception. It takes its cue from what may be thought of as secular forms of transition ideologies, like the "gospels" of Progress and Manifest Destiny, which were used to justify and explain the westward expansion of the United States as a young nation. These narratives have always informed American activity and America's civil religion with the notion that there does exist an especially favored relationship between God and the United States of America, the "city on a hill" and "light of the world." The leaving behind of what is familiar to embrace the unknown would leave people with a need to make sense of the journey and, most of all, of the subsequent experience, especially if it was particularly positive (or negative). For some people, religion provides the most compelling set of conceptual tools for this task. As a relatively young nation, American society has always been fashioned and refashioned by large-scale movements of people, from immigration from other nations to intranational population shifts to varying degrees of social and economic mobility. To have a doctrine that provides meaning to the transitory nature of late modern life would seem to make perfect sense.

These ideologies support the belief of those who, having chosen to move from one location to another—be it a physical movement, a movement in social class position, switching from one denominational affiliation to another or to an independent religious affiliation, or a more metaphoric shift in perception and worldview—have somehow "progressed" beyond the level of those they have left behind. America's self-image includes the implied idea that, like Abraham of the Bible, those who have struck out for the unknown are somehow more deserving of the blessings bestowed on them by God as a reward for their faith. It is an indication of their favor with God that he would speak to them, and a testament to their obedience to his leading that they would "step out on faith," into the unknown, and be blessed as a result. The Faith Message embodies these ways of thinking that have long been part of the American self-image relative to other nations of the world.

But the Faith Message presupposes the freedoms, rights, and privileges that Americans have and that people in most other countries do not and seems to be particularly well suited to sensibilities shaped in this context. Therefore, although it is not isolated to the United States, its implications are not the same in this national-cultural context as they would be in those of other nations. Consonant with the historical moment during which it began to emerge, the Word of Faith Movement's emphasis on *conspicuous* consumption as an act of one's faith resonates with the prosperity and access to wealth that has been such a part of the life experiences of many who are part of the post–World War II Baby Boom generation, so many of whom are the movement's leaders and who make up a large part of its clientele. Above all, the Faith Message, for all its apparent excesses and eccentricities, represents a particularly American way of thinking about the nature of spirituality and faith, what we believe is our nation's favored relationship to God, and our privileged status relative to the rest of the world. This doctrine is another contemporary, Christianized version of secular, civil religious currents present in the American worldview from its earliest days as a nation.

Some Parting Thoughts on the Word of Faith Movement

The Word of Faith Movement is a phenomenon that embodies some of the ways in which preexisting sacred and profane concerns can come together and articulate in new and interesting forms. But what will be the fate of this particular brand of Christianity in the twenty-first century? It appears likely that the Word of Faith Movement will continue to grow in popularity and influence, both in the United States and abroad. One reason for this expected growth is that it entices people to move from denominational churches to independent churches that promise to better serve the needs and desires of the individual. On the surface, these churches appear to be less concerned with enforcement of the obligation of the believer to the church by emphasizing what religion and spirituality can do *for them*. The movement attracts new members by its insistence on being "a new revelation" from God that promises personal fulfillment, including a materially abundant life, the knowledge of which has been withheld from believers by their denominational leaders either out of ignorance or from the desire to keep them poor and dependent. Because of its mutability and because there is no ideological or structural center, the movement and its ministries can combine elements from various realms of culture in order to attract new members by providing something they recognize as familiar but repackaged and redefined as "new and improved" charismatic Christianity. These churches tend to grow very quickly as a result of the novelty and new sense of freedom from the established religious traditions many people have grown up with. The excitement of television cameras, the inclusion of various other elements borrowed from secular popular culture in the teaching and in the services, and the linkage to the scriptural promise of material prosperity all make it seem as though this movement is truly a "move of God" that is not to be missed if one is to remain in the center of his will.

The Word of Faith Movement offers a sense of personal, individual *empowerment* to those who have been left out of the mainstream of economic and social life, thus making it attractive to the poor who don't want to stay poor in America and elsewhere, particularly in developing nations. This is helped by its ability to synthesize elements of local religious traditions (for example, in Seoul, Korea, where the world's largest church is a Word of Faith movement church). At its heart this is a movement based upon a doctrine that gives meaning to socioeconomic mobility. For those who have not yet been upwardly mobile, the doctrine supplies explanations (such as their being "between blessings"). But for those who have become more prosperous or are in the process of becoming so, this belief system is an important conceptual vehicle supporting their efforts. And this outpost of the electronic church has extensively exploited the mass media to spread its message.

As an unintended consequence of its relative success at drawing from popular culture and making use of telecommunications media, other movements—even some with denominational affiliations—have begun to adopt some of the characteristics once associated primarily if not solely with the movement. It is, therefore, not as distinctive as it was once thought to be, and the "novelty factor" that attracted denominational switchers in the past has begun to diminish. In the past 17 years since I first become acquainted with the movement, I (as well as numerous others I have talked with) have noticed that it is becoming increasingly difficult to distinguish Faith Message teachings and practices from those commonly associated with some of the denominational churches. There was a time when a repeated phrase like "Turn with me in your Bible to [a particular scripture]," with the assumption that people actually brought Bibles to church with them and knew their way around them, would have been a clue that one was in a Word church. Such multiple, back-to-back scriptural references, with the minister "teaching" on the meaning and application of each scripture and how it supports his or her overall thesis, would have been seen as one of the conventions that set the Word of Faith Movement churches off from denominational churches, especially within Holiness/Pentecostal circles. But today some non–Word of Faith churches have adopted this emphasis on and method of *teaching* scripture in the Sunday morning services.

Today, it is not as clear where the Word of Faith Movement's beliefs and teaching end and those more characteristic of certain denominational churches begin. Many contemporary denominational churches today are appropriating other conventions formerly associated with groups like the Word of Faith. One such convention is the form of congregational singing called "praise and worship," frequently cited by my respondents, in which a "praise team" with microphones stands before the congregation and leads up-tempo "praise" songs to contemporary musical accompaniment, usually with a large instrumental backup group. After the period of "praise" comes the "worship" segment, with slower music, more contemplative in tone. I have been in churches with the denominational marker "Church of God in. Christ," in which the service included praise and worship, while retaining the style of teaching mentioned earlier, *along with* the sermonic *preaching* tradition, from which many in the mainstream of the Word of Faith Movement have attempted to distance themselves.

One final example illustrates this change. There was a time when the Word of Faith Movement seemed to be most closely associated with the "Name it and claim it" doctrine. But in the last 15 years or so this idea, and the practice of verbally giving voice to a desired outcome, seem to have gained wider acceptance and use. To offer another musical example: some contemporary gospel songs express sentiments like God wants you to "have it all." The lyrics of a recent release by a well-known gospel singer contain that very statement. Some of the claims made by the Word of Faith Movement, especially within the African American community a decade ago, then considered outrageous, now seem to be gaining wider currency. The talk show hosts Oprah Winfrey and Phil McGraw, "Dr. Phil," regularly use the phrase "Name it and claim it" in talking to guests about how to make changes in their lives, and they are not necessarily using the phrase in a religious content. All these things suggest that what were formerly considered the excesses and eccentricities of the Word of Faith Movement and other groups like it are becoming increasingly a part of mainstream culture, from which many of its elements came in the first place. And so those attracted to novelty and "edginess" may have to go elsewhere to find or create it.

This diffusion is, to an extent, due to the fact that some from within the Word of Faith Movement are coming full circle, as more than one of the respondents in this study has indicated. When they leave, they are taking with them what they have learned in the movement churches: how to study the Bible, positive confession, knowing who they are in Christ and the awareness of the benefits of that identity. Some people are going back to denominational churches that have a long, rich historical tradition, rather than remaining in Word of Faith Movement churches that market themselves as iconoclastic and the carriers of a new revelation of God's redemption, marketing in which a primary value rests in *not* being denominational. For some who are still heavily invested in those older traditions, the novelty of the Word of Faith Movement gradually wears off, and they grow weary of hearing that their roots were inferior and that this movement's new conventions are somehow less limiting and *conventional* than those of the "first church."

Television's role in spreading and popularizing the Faith Message cannot be overstated. It is important to recognize the extent to which television exposure, which seems to grow steadily, makes certain elements of the message seem less localized and more a part of the landscape of larger contemporary evangelical Christian culture. There seems to be a degree of homogenization at work as a result of the pervasive use of televised religious broadcasting. One can see and hear what other ministers are doing, and even see how large their sanctuaries are, how large their choirs are, what the decor of their church looks like; you can see what they are doing and teaching even without having to be physically present in the setting. You can also pick and choose from among these elements in forming and re-forming your own church, its teachings, and physical environment. If people both can have access to the Faith Message and retain a sense of denominational history and honored traditions, which the Word of Faith Movement seeks to do away with (or at least deemphasize), there is less of a need for people to switch denominational affiliations than there might have appeared to be in times past. This process by which the cultural forms of marginalized groups is appropriated and co-opted, becoming part of mainstream culture, is not unique to this movement or to religion. This is a large part of the dynamism of American culture.

Some traditional social science conceptions of religiosity have focused on institutionally prescribed forms of observance like prayer, going to confession, rates of church attendance, or attitudes on certain social and political issues and their effects on voting behavior. But many people believe their religious faith should determine even the most basic, mundane aspects of their lives and shape the choices they routinely make. For these people the purchase of a certain type or color of vehicle or the decisions whether or not to submit an insurance claim for a stolen car or whether to take medication at the first sign of common cold symptoms become exercises in and opportunities for applying their faith. Rather than a static abstraction, people's faith is an ongoing process that is embodied in real situations. The "everyday theologians" we have met in this book allow us to witness and to appreciate some of the complexities and nuances involved in this ongoing process of making sense of doctrine and "working out your own salvation" in the context of everyday life.

Notes

INTRODUCTION

1. All scriptural references are from the King James Version (KJV).

2. Although the movement's origins are in the United States, like many other forms of evangelical Christianity, the Word of Faith Movement has been successful in other regions of the world, with many United States–based ministries having "outreaches" or extensions in any number of foreign countries as well as U.S. territories.

3. Price received an honorary diploma from Hagin's Rhema Bible Training Center (1976), and as tribute to his influence on Price, one of the buildings on the campus of Crenshaw Christian Center bore Hagin's name for several years. But recently, as Price has been engaged in a series of teachings and books attacking racism in the Christian church, the relationship between the two men changed. When Kenneth Hagin, Jr., preached against interracial marriage, Price took issue. And when Hagin the elder defended his son's position, Price felt compelled to sever ties with his former spritual leader, even going so far as to having Hagin's name removed from the building on the Crenshaw Christian Center campus.

4. Dan R. McConnell, *A Different Gospel: Biblical and Historical Insights into the Word of Faith Movement* (Peabody, MA: Hendrickson Publishers, 1988), p. xix.

5. Some of the titles of Kenyon's work in which his theological perspectives are explicated in his own words include: Don Gossett and E. W. Kenyon, *The Power of Your Words: Walking with God by Agreeing with God* (New Kensington, PA: Whitaker House, 1977); and all of the following by E. W. Kenyon, *Identification: A Romance in Redemption* (Lynnwood, WA: Kenyon's

Gospel Publishing Society, 1941); *The Father and His Family* (Lynnwood, WA: Kenyon's Gospel Publishing Society, 1998); *The Two Kinds of Faith: Faith's Secret Revealed* (Lynnwood, WA: Kenyon's Gospel Publishing Society, 1998); *The Two Kinds of Knowledge* (Lynnwood, WA: Kenyon's Gospel Publishing Society, 1998).

6. *The KJV New Testament Greek Lexicon,* available online at: www.biblestudy tools.net/Lexicons/Greek/grk.cgi?number=4487&version=kjv. The word "rhema" (originally "rema") is used in the New Testament a total of 67 times. It is the word and concept used in the original scriptural phrase "word of faith" (Romans 10:8), from which Hagin's newsletter/magazine takes its name, and this is the source of the larger movement's name as well. The website is run by Crosswalk.com a for-profit religious corporation that includes a variety of Bible study tools as well as other goods and services to support the Christian lifestyle. The Greek lexicon used on this website is based on the following two references in particular: Joseph Thayer, *Thayer's Greek-English Lexicon of the New Testament: Coded with Strong's Concordance Numbers* (Peabody, MA: Hendrickson Publishers, Reissued edition, 1996); William Smith, *Smith's Bible Dictionary* (Peabody, MA: Hendrickson Publishers, Revised edition, 1990). These files are public domain.

7. In his book *The Father and His Family* (1998), Kenyon writes that "Christianity is a legal document" (191) and that God conferred upon humankind certain legal rights that through the Fall of Man were forfeited to Satan. The believer who knows who he or she is can then reclaim his or her God-given authority over Satan and triumph over sickness and disease, poverty, and any other negative circumstance.

8. John Avanzini, "Was Jesus Poor?" *Believer's Voice of Victory,* January 1996, p. 4.

9. On this basis, many in the Christian community consider the Word of Faith Movement and its doctrine to be yet another example of the ways evangelical Christianity has capitulated to the pressures to conform to the larger culture in which it is embedded. Others who follow McConnell's lead are: John Mac Arthur, *Charismatic Chaos* (Grand Rapids, MI: Zondervan Publishing House, 1992), Dave Hunt, *Occult Invasion* (Eugene, OR: Harvest House, 1998), Hank Hanegraaf, *Christianity in Crisis* (Eugene, OR: Harvest House, 1997), and John Ankerberg and John Weldon, *The Facts on the Faith Movement* (Eugene, OR: Harvest House, 1993). Perhaps one of the most important of the movement's critics is Jim Bakker, a former proponent of the Faith Message who has written a book criticizing the movement and its teachings, *Prosperity and the Coming Apocalypse* (Nashville, TN: Thomas Nelson, 1998). In the book, written after his release from prison where he served a term for embezzlement, Bakker says that he once taught that it was God's will for believers to prosper financially, but that during his imprisonment God showed him that what he and so many others had been teaching as part of the Word of Faith Movement was wrong and that Christians should seek to simplify their lives, eschewing the desire for material wealth as they prepare for the return of Christ. Bruce Barron, *The Health and Wealth Gospel* (Dawner's Grove, IL: InterVarsity Press, 1987), provides a much more balanced analysis of the doctrine of the Word of Faith Movement, and I recommend it to those interested in finding out more detail about the specifics of the doctrine's origins, its basic

tenets, and formative personalities. This book, however, published by an sectarian press, does still focus on the theological debate concerning the validity and legitimacy of the doctrine.

10. Stanley M. Burgess, Gary B. McGee, and Patrick H. Alexander, eds., *Dictionary of Pentecostal and Charismatic Movements* (1988); Trinity Broadcast Network is available online at: http://www.tbn.org/whois/.

11. Trinity Broadcast Network enjoys an overwhelming presence in Central and South America, the Caribbean, and Brazil. It is throughout this region of Central and South America that TBN has its greatest concentration and, presumably (or potentially) its greatest audience. It is also noteworthy that TBN has affiliates in at least 200 broadcasting areas (not including cable systems) throughout Europe and the former Soviet Union. It is surprising to see the extent to which evangelical TBN is concentrated in Italy, what would presumably be a predominately Roman Catholic market.

12. The ICFM website is at: http://www.icfm.org.

13. These figures are valid as of July 2002. Lists of registered members of ICFM are *not exhaustive*; there are some rather glaring absences. Among those not listed among ICFM members are some of the movement's most prominent figures, such as Kenneth E. Hagin, Sr. of Rhema Bible Church (Tulsa, Oklahoma), Frederick K. C. Price of Crenshaw Christian Center (Los Angeles, California), and Paul Yonggi Cho of Yoido Full Gospel Church (Seoul, Korea). Each of these ministers have megachurches, Dr. Cho's church reports that it is the largest church in the world with more than 736,000 members (according to the most recent membership figures published on the church's website: http://english.fgtv.com/).

14. From "We Are the Fellowship" page, FICWFM website: http://www.ficwfm.org/start.htm.

15. Information on actual numbers of member congregations and their geographical distribution is not as complete for FICWFM as for ICFM and RMAI. My attempts at gathering this type of demographic information from the organization were unsuccessful.

CHAPTER I

1. In *"Greater Than the Former": Observations on the Construction of Community within the Pentecostal Tradition*, paper presented at the annual meeting of the American Sociological Association, Washington, DC, August 19–23, 1995, I addressed in greater detail the process by which individual believers become transformed into a television audience in the setting. Through various types of behavioral instruction, they learn to do their part as a "team" in the collective management of a corporate impression for the benefit of those watching at home and enjoying a disembodied experience of being part of the community of believers.

2. See Christian Smith's *American Evangelicals: Embattled and Thriving* (Chicago: University of Chicago Press, 1998) for a discussion of his "subcultural theory of reli-

gious strength." Chapters 4 and 5 present a theoretical model that purports to explain the importance for contemporary evangelicals, in a religiously pluralistic environment, of creating an identity based on their sense of their group's distinctiveness in lifestyle and values relative to those who do not share their faith. This subcultural identity is, according to this model, key to understanding the strong attraction and subsequent allegiance of self-identified evangelicals in the face of so many contemporary challenges to their beliefs from the larger culture. Although his discussion is addressed to a research question and population that is indirectly related to those in this book, his theory is nevertheless instructive to helping us understanding how important the Word of Faith Movement's emphasis on their members' having an identity as the people who "know who they are in Christ" and that that identity serves as the basis for their subsequent beliefs and practices, especially those concerning material prosperity.

3. In *Truth and Method* (New York: Crossroads, 1989), the German philosopher Hans Georg Gadamer referred to this background, using the concept of "horizon." One's horizon is fluid, constantly being shaped and reshaped, and is based on past and present experiences that then become part of the distinctive contextual, interpretive framework that each individual brings to the experience of any new object, text, concept, or experience (or the same at different times, contexts, and so on). Also see Joel C. Weinsheimer, *Godamer's Hermeneutics: A Reading of* Truth and Method (New Haven, NJ: Yale University Press, 1985).

CHAPTER 3

Parts of this chapter have been adapted from earlier research in this setting reported in a paper presented at the annual meeting of the American Sociological Association, Washington, DC, August 19–23, 1995.

1. In addition to not using the real names of any of the people (except for visiting "stars" who are seen on television daily), the neighborhood, and the church in which this study took place have been changed in order to protect the privacy and anonymity of the congregation and its leaders. I have also omitted the names of local newspapers.

2. The 2000 Census Data have not been completed; however according to estimates, the situation remained relatively unchanged.

3. So as not to disclose the church's actual name, I have not given the name of the article, the author, or the newspaper (and date) in which it appeared.

4. Bringing paper/pen and taking notes may not always be explicitly stated as "the right thing to do," but it is certainly the norm in both the churches in which this study was done. Speakers will often instruct the congregation to write certain things in their Bibles or "in their notes" and then wait until it appears that most people have finished writing to proceed.

5. Observing the practices of more than one traditional, denominationally-affiliated, church, I have seen and personally experienced instances in which the mere

expression of *desire* or *intent* to become a member was all that was needed for the pastor (or other church official) to introduce the new member to the congregation in a subsequent service and have their name added to the membership roll.

6. This emphasis on intellectually knowing, taking classes, studying laws, principles and formulae are part of one example of the type of rationalization that James D. Hunter, *American Evangelicalism* (New Bruswick: Rutgers University Press, 1983), noted as characteristic of contemporary Evangelical religion.

7. Frederick K. C. Price, *Prosperity on God's Terms* (Los Angeles: Ever Increasing Faith Ministries, 1990), 11.

8. Hunter, *American Evangelicalism*, chapter 6, discussing some of the trends in conservative Protestantism in the decades since the 1960s, stated the fact that in contemporary evangelicalism, the old-style hellfire-and- brimstone message has been effectively replaced with one that focuses on psychological (and in this case, financial) well-being, based upon the codification and rationalization of the message into laws, principles, and formulae. This aspect of contemporary spirituality is certainly to be found in this ministry and its ways of thinking about and teaching religion.

9. In "Sacrifice of Praise" (1996), Timothy J. Nelson discussed the role of emotional display in Black worship services not as occurring "naturally," as has been long thought, but as subject to the power relations within the church. When those with the power to define the range of acceptable behaviors in the worship service do so in such as way as to sanction freedom of ecstatic display, then it becomes the norm; on the other hand, negative sanctions follow when the rules concerning appropriate emotional display prohibit certain behaviors, and those who engage in them become subject to the pressure to conform to the prevailing definition of the situation. Hence some Black churches have more emotionally expressive services than others; it is a function of the behavioral rules at work in the setting.

CHAPTER 4

1. The Security Ministry is a relatively recent addition to the roster of departments making up the division of labor in the church. These individuals, who are mostly but not exclusively men, serve as bodyguards for the pastor, his family, and whoever else is in their party when they traveling; they are part of his "entourage." They operate in ways that are not dissimilar to what we've commonly come to associate with the Secret Service as they "cover" the President of the United States and his party. During church services they keep watch over the proceedings from a number of locations around the auditorium, communicating with each other via small microphones and earpieces. After the services they take up positions around the pastor (and his wife) and regulate the flow of people who would approach him to shake his hand or interact with him in some other way. If someone appears intent on doing harm to the pastor, the responsibility of these members of the security ministry is to assess the situation and act accordingly. For some people who have been members of the ministry for many years—when the church was much smaller and the pastor more

"approachable"—the presence of these "secret service men" is off-putting and nega-tively symbolic of how the environment of the church has changed as the church has grown.

CHAPTER 5

1. The institutional centrality of the Black Church in the experience of African Americans has been well established and affirmed in the work of a number of schol-ars including the following: Arthur H. Fauset, *Black Gods of the Metropolis* (Philadel-phia, University of Pennsylvania Press, 1944); St. Clair Drake and Horace R. Cayton, *Black Metropolis: A Study of Negro Life in an Urban City* (New York: Harcourt, Brace and Company, 1945); Carter G. Woodson, *The History of the Negro Church* (Washing-ton, DC: The Associated Publishers, 1945); E. Frazier Franklin, *The Negro Church in America* (New York: Schocken Books, 1964); Benjamin E. Mays and Joseph W. Nichol-son, *The Negro's Church* (New York: Russell and Russell, 1969); and C. Eric Lincoln and Lawrence H. Mamiya, *The Black Church in the African American Experience* (Dur-ham: Duke University Press, 1990).

2. Larry J. Murphy, J. Gordon Melton, and Gary Ward, eds., *Encyclopedia of Afri-can American Religions* (New York: Garland, 1993).

3. For more on Father Divine, see Robert Weisbrot, *Father Divine* (1983), and Ar-thur H. Fausett, *Black Gods of the Metropolis* (1944).

4. See Murphy, Melton, and Ward, *Encyclopedia of African American Religions*.

5. Dr. H. Lewis Johnson (b. 1890), a female minister and founder of Antioch As-sociation of Metaphysical Science in Detroit in 1932, was one of the first African American religious leaders to appropriate New Thought teachings and is therefore a predecessor to Johnnie Colemon.

6. Murphy, Melton, and Ward, *Encyclopedia of African American Religions*.

7. It is possible and likely that Hagin heard of these teachings not directly from E. W. Kenyon but through some of these New Thought teachers who were more his contemporaries and who also broadcast their messages on the radio. Reverend Ike was one of the first Black ministers to be seen on a regular nationwide television show, and, according to Murphy, Melton, and Ward, *Encyclopedia of African American Religions,* "his work represents a major inroad of New Thought into the Black com-munity" (247).

8. Today's Word of Faith Movement shares a variety of characteristics with the groups mentioned in this section, particularly with respect to its presence in the Afri-can American religious community. For a more thorough explanation and analysis of these prior movements, please see Hans A. Baer and Merrill Singer, *African American Religion: Varieties of Protest and Accommodation* (Knoxville: University of Tennessee Press, 2002). In chapter 6 Baer and Singer situated the movements of Reverence Ike and of Jonnie Colemon (along with Black Spiritualists) in the category of the "thau-maturcial sect," defined as those groups that "emphasize the reordering of one's pres-ent health or social condition through magico-religious rituals and esoteric knowl-edge" (p. 183). They go on to say "characteristically, thaumaturgical sects unabashedly

emphasize the acquisition of the "good life" along with its worldly pleasures" (p. 183). Certainly, the Word of Faith Movement of today fits this description and in the context of African American religious history is appropriately placed.

9. Tomika DePriest and Joyce Jones, "Economic Development through the Church," *Black Enterprise*, February 1997, p. 195.

10. DePriest and Jones, "Economic Development," p. 196.

11. DePriest and Jones, "Economic Development," p. 196.

12. Harris, "Redefining Kingdom Business."

13. Harris, "Redefining Kingdom Business," p. 38.

14. Daniel B. Wood, "Black Churches as Big Players in Urban Renewal," *Christian Science Monitor*, electronic ed., January 25, 2001.

15. Teresa E. Hairston, "One Nation United in Faith," *Gospel Today*, July 2001.

16. Teresa E. Hairston, "Redefining Kingdom Business: Churches Possessing the Land,"*Gospel Today*, May/June 2000, p. 44.

17. Members of this 12-member Board of Governors include: Ray, T. D. Jakes, G. E. Patterson, Paul S. Morton, Eddie Long, Carlton Pearson, the late Mack Timberlake, J. Delano Ellis, Floyd Flake, and Charles Blake.

18. Harris, "Redefining."

19. Nehemiah Corporation of America website: http://www.nehemiahcorp.org/.

20. "The New Mega Churches," *Ebony*, December 2001.

21. Murphy, Melton, and Ward, *Encyclopedia of African American Religions*.

22. Thomas J. Lueck, "Deal Is Close on Landmark Church Near Central Park," *New York Times*, March 27, 2004.

CONCLUSION

1. Donald E. Miller, *Reinventing American Protestantism: Christianity in the New Millennium* (Berkeley: University of California Press, 1997).

2. Christian Smith, *American Evangelicalism: Embattled and Thriving* (Chicago: University of Chicago Press, 1998).

3. The concept of ideology of transition comes from the sociologist of religion Thomas F. O'Dea, *Sociology and the Study of Religion: Theory, Research, and Interpretation* (New York: Basic Books, 1970).

Index